To the Glory and Praise of God

OPEN DOORS

Fred W. Scott

Trilogy Christian Publishers
A Wholly Owned Subsidiary of Trinity Broadcasting Network
2442 Michelle Drive
Tustin, CA 92780
Copyright © 2020 by Fred W. Scott
All Scripture quotations, unless otherwise noted, taken from THE HOLY BIBLE, NEW INTERNATIONAL VERSION®, NIV® Copyright © 1973, 1978, 1984, 2011 by Biblica, Inc.® Used by permission. All rights reserved worldwide.
Scripture quotations marked (KJV) taken from The Holy Bible, King James Version. Cambridge Edition: 1769.
All rights reserved, including the right to reproduce this book or portions thereof in any form whatsoever.
For information, address Trilogy Christian Publishing Rights Department, 2442 Michelle Drive, Tustin, Ca 92780.
Trilogy Christian Publishing/ TBN and colophon are trademarks of Trinity Broadcasting Network.
For information about special discounts for bulk purchases, please contact Trilogy Christian Publishing.
Manufactured in the United States of America

10 9 8 7 6 5 4 3 2 1
Library of Congress Cataloging-in-Publication Data is available.
ISBN 978-1-64773-398-8
ISBN 978-1-64773-399-5 (ebook)

DEDICATION

This book is dedicated to Dr. James H. Gillespie.

The late Dr. James H. Gillespie was my mentor. His guidance, support, and encouragement during my graduate studies and as a fellow faculty member in the Department of Microbiology and Immunology shaped my career in veterinary medicine. Without his vision to start the feline infectious diseases program at the Cornell University College of Veterinary Medicine, I probably would not have ventured into the feline infectious disease field, and the Cornell Feline Health Center probably would not have been founded. God used this giant in veterinary virology to greatly improve the health and welfare of several animal species within His animal kingdom, including dogs, cats, cattle, and horses.

Table of Contents

Foreword   9

Chapter 1 —Setting the Stage   13
    Glory Where Glory is Due
    His Mighty Acts
    Doors

Chapter 2 —Testimony of the Saving Grace of Jesus Christ   17
    The Narrow Gate
    Why Me, Lord?

Chapter 3 —God's Grace   29
    The Call Home
    Gary Bolton
    Evolution vs. Creation
    Knowledge to Wisdom
    Peace that Surpasses All Understanding

Chapter 4 —The Road to Veterinary Medicine   45
    Career Decision
    Undergraduate Pre-Veterinary Training
    College of Veterinary Medicine

Chapter 5 —Veterinary Medicine ~ The Early Years   59
    Rutland Veterinary Clinic

Potential Free Large Animal Practice
Legendary Dr. Fox, Sage Advice, and a Wonderful Open Door
Plum Island Animal Disease Laboratory
Postdoctoral Graduate Studies
Bovine Winter Dysentery Thread
Open Door to Feline Infectious Disease Research
Research on Feline Panleukopenia

Chapter 6 —Faculty Member ~ Cornell University College of Veterinary Medicine   83

Faculty Position
Research
Bovine Winter Dysentery
Feline Panleukopenia
Adoption Shelter Feline Vaccines
Feline Respiratory Vaccines
Disinfectants vs. Feline Viruses
Feline Infectious Peritonitis
Teaching
Continuing Education for Practicing Veterinarian
Feline Infectious Disease Elective
Virology and Viral Diseases Core Course
Teaching Slide Preparation
Curriculum
Graduate Students

Chapter 7 —Cornell Feline Health Center   135
    History
    Concept: Memorandum for the Record
    Where to Start?
    John Saidla
    James Richards
    Interim Director

Chapter 8 —Veterinary Associations   147
    American Association of Feline Practitioners
    American Veterinary Medical Association
    American Animal Hospital Association
    American College of Veterinary Microbiology
    Conference of Research Workers in Animal Diseases
    Christian Veterinary Fellowship

Chapter 9 —Honors and Awards   155

Chapter 10 —Childhood and Early Years   159
    Early Education
    Church
    Early Jobs

Chapter 11 —Family   173
    Heritage
    Spouse
    Children
    Grandchildren
    Great-Grandchildren

Chapter 12 —God as Realtor 183

Addendums 195
    Sayings to Live By
    Abbreviations

Afterword 201
    Glory
    OPEN DOOR in Heaven

FOREWORD

As I look back over the past eighty-plus years of my life, I am utterly amazed at the blessings the Lord showered upon this naive farm kid from a small town in western Massachusetts. My family and I have been blessed beyond measure!

The Lord opened doors, closed doors, and directed my path within the veterinary profession in ways that I could not comprehend at the time, and to heights that would have been impossible to accomplish with my own limited abilities. I am totally convinced that any achievements I was able to attain were not attained by my efforts alone, but by the Lord's directing, guiding, and opening opportunities for His glory and righteousness. I believe the Lord was orchestrating situations and placing me in front of open door after open door as this small-town farm kid from a high school class of seven moved through undergraduate college, to veterinary college, to practicing veterinarian, to post-graduate studies, and to university professor.

Look back over the course of your life. If you're a child of God, you'll undoubtedly see how God opened doors, closed doors, directed and redirected, ruled and overruled, and led in paths of righteousness for His name's sake. —David Jeremiah. *Today's Turning Poin*t. August 24, 2016

The first thirty-seven years of my life, and the first eleven years of my veterinary career, I was not a believer —I did not have a personal relationship with Jesus Christ. Yet, He still opened doors, closed doors, and directed my path without me realizing it.

Then in 1973, shortly after my promotion to Associate Professor of Virology with tenure within the Cornell University College of Veterinary Medicine, Jesus Christ dramatically opened the most magnificent door and gently guided me to a personal relationship with Him. His Amazing Grace gave me an entirely new perspective on life, my family, and my career!

    What I did not realize, or even have a slight clue of, at the time early in my career was the plan the Lord had for me in veterinary medicine and in the area of feline infectious diseases. I was interested in bovine viral diseases, not feline. One night more than fifty years after starting my feline research, I was quietly reflecting on just how this occurred, and how the sharing of the research information on feline panleukopenia with private veterinary practitioners across the country came about. It hit me like a flash! The Holy Spirit clearly said to me:

> *This is the plan I had for you. I placed you in the epicenter of feline research to conduct re-*

> *search on feline panleukopenia, then to share these research results with veterinarians across the country in order to completely control feline panleukopenia.*

Wow!

As I relate the accomplishments and experiences as a veterinarian and Cornell University faculty member, I do so not to show "how great thou art" or to say, "Look what I have accomplished." Rather, I do so to show how the Lord was able to take this farm boy and transition him into a cog in this wonderful profession of veterinary medicine, and hopefully to provide some benefits to the profession and the welfare of a portion of His animal kingdom. I have no false illusions about my own grandeur, but I do have a tremendous awareness of the grace, glory, and greatness of our Lord, and how He can use a simple and imperfect person to accomplish His amazing purposes—how He can open doors that would seem to be impossible to open!

So, I invite the reader to come along with me as the Lord opens the door of my life to reveal the amazing things He has done. To God be the glory!

CHAPTER 1

Setting the Stage

Glory Where Glory Is Due

Most Protestant Christians are familiar with what is referred to as the Common Doxology which begins, 'Praise God, from whom all blessings flow: praise Him, all creatures here below.' It was composed in 1674 as the final verse of two hymns used in morning and evening worship at England's Winchester College. There is a world of theology and counsel bound up in the phrase, 'from whom all blessings flow.'

And there is a world of danger in forgetting that God is the source of all we have: victory, strength, blessing, success—it all comes from Him. The danger is that we might accumulate credit unto ourselves for our victories and success instead of giving credit and glory to Him. That is, we put ourselves in the place of God as the source of all that is good. Everything can be traced back to God. Yes, we may use our intelligence and skill in daily life—but where does intelligence and skill come from? As the Doxology says, we 'praise God from whom all blessings flow.' Some blessings come directly and some indirectly. But He is the source of them all.

Make sure to give credit, glory, and thanks to God for what He enables you to accomplish in life. —Dr. David Jeremiah. *Today's Turning Point.* August 11, 2017

His Mighty Acts

Knowing the details of God's work is crucial to giving him praise . . . . God tells us repeatedly in the Bible to remember His mighty acts. That involves two crucial steps: You have to know the acts themselves. And you have to recognize them as coming from God. . . You can enhance your sense of praise by daring to give God public credit for what you believe deep in your heart He has actually done. —Joel Belz. *World Magazine.* February 2, 2019

Doors

Our schemes often go awry. God's never do. Look back over the course of your life. If you're a child of God, you'll undoubtedly see how God opened doors, closed doors, directed and redirected, ruled and overruled, and led in paths of righteousness for His name's sake. —David Jeremiah, *Today's Turning Point*, August 24, 2016

Sometimes God makes better choices for us than we could ever have made for ourselves. —Jennifer Hudson Taylor, from *Highland Blessings*, quoted in Guideposts, December 2016, p.14

Ask and it will be given to you; seek and you will find; knock and the door will be opened to you. For everyone who asks receives; he who seeks finds; and to him who knocks, the door will be opened. —Matthew 7:7-8

7These are the words of him who is holy and true, who holds the key of David. What he opens, no one can shut; and what he shuts, no one can open. 8I know your deeds. See, I have placed before you an open door that no one can shut. —Revelation 3:7-8

Here I am! I stand at the door and knock. If anyone hears my voice and opens the door, I will come in and eat with him, and he with me. —Revelation 3:20

After this I looked, and there before me was a door standing open in heaven. —Revelation 4:1

CHAPTER 2

Testimony of the Saving Grace of Jesus Christ

I grew up on a small dairy farm in western Massachusetts during the midst of the Great Depression and World War II. Times were tough, and we were with little money but plenty to eat since we grew everything on the farm. Mine was a close-knit family, with two older brothers (Ed and Roger or "Bud"), an older sister (Gladys or "Scottie"), and wonderful, supportive parents, Clifton, and Mildred Scott.

Our family was very much into sports, namely baseball and basketball. My dad was a high school teacher and baseball coach before he went into farming, and he and my older brothers taught me the fine details of sports. I played baseball and basketball throughout school, and sports participation and observation have remained high in my priorities throughout life.

My family attended church regularly, and I attended Sunday school in the local Congregational Church. It probably occurred and I just was not listening, but I do not remember ever hearing about a personal relationship with Jesus Christ either from my parents or in church or Sunday school. When I got into high school and got involved in playing baseball and basketball for both the high school and the local town teams, church worship had little attraction to me. When I attended college at the University of Massachusetts, church and worship seemed unnecessary. I had better things to do on Sundays. For nearly twenty years—after graduating high school until the age of thirty-seven—I did not darken the door of a church unless it was for a wedding or funeral.

My early professional life could be characterized as a series of goals to be accomplished but with no certainty that they would be accomplished: getting into college, getting accepted into veterinary college at Cornell, graduating from veterinary college, becoming established within a private veterinary practice in Rutland, Vermont, applying for a National Institutes of Health postdoctoral fellowship, acceptance into graduate school, completing my PhD at Cornell, obtaining a faculty position at Cornell, and establishing a successful research program. My focus was on these goals and what the successful attainment of each goal would bring. My focus was not on my family, and certainly not on anything connected with religion. After accomplishing many of my goals, I became caught up in "the world"— looking for more material things. After all, I had been somewhat "deprived," or so I thought, in my earlier years, and it was time to cash in on my rewards.

My wife, Lois, grew up on the neighboring farm, and we rode the same school bus to elementary and high school. In fact, she and I are third cousins, with the same great-great-grandparents who owned a neighboring farm. We were part of a square dance exhibition team, and we began to date in high school. We were married after my junior year at UMass, a small wedding at the home of Lois's parents. We thought it was hypocritical to have a church wedding when neither of us had had anything to do with the church for several years. Lois worked at various jobs, and I had numerous part-time jobs to support the family while I finished my senior year at UMass and the next four years of veterinary college at Cornell. We were blessed with two wonderful sons, Duane, and John, during these years of college, and a third delightful son, Raymond, arrived during my first year of graduate school. I was a student with no regular employment for eight of the first eleven years of our marriage. Talk about stress on a marriage! Lois continued to be the faithful homemaker, providing the glue that held our family together while I was off "doing my thing professionally."

During the early 1970s, Lois began searching, knowing instinctively that there was more to life than we were experiencing. She began to investigate the Mormon religion, attracted to what she saw in the families of Mormons that we encountered. In the spring of 1973, she was invited to attend a women's tea with a neighbor whose husband was a graduate student at Cornell. At this tea, the gospel of Jesus Christ was presented to her in a clear and concise fashion such as she had never heard before. Together with the testimonies presented by some of the women in attendance, this event had a substantial impact on her. A few days later she committed her life to the Lord.

Things at home changed from that point on. Lois desperately wanted to share with me the "good news" she had found. She began to attend Bible studies, listened to Christian radio, and all sorts of "religious" books and materials began to appear around the house. I wanted no part of it! One day she said to me: "This is a great book; you've got to read it." She handed me Hal Lindsey's 1972 book *Satan is Alive and Well on Planet Earth.* I took one look at the title and retorted: "You have got to be kidding!" I slammed the book on the table and walked out the door. Just hearing Christian radio was enough to double my blood pressure and send me out to the garden to hoe weeds—that garden got more hoeing that summer than any garden I have had before or since.

This religious "stuff" drove a huge wedge into an already shaky marriage. I continued my quest of the world, and things continued to get worse at home. Finally, in a rather dramatic fashion—I do not know how, the Lord made it crystal clear to me that this marriage was over, and I did not want it to be over.

At this point, I put my stubbornness aside and listened to Lois. She quietly shared with me the gospel of Jesus Christ—that we all are sinners, that our sin separates us from Christ, and that Christ died for our sins. Only by admitting that we are sinners, asking God for forgiveness of those sins, and asking Jesus Christ to come into our lives, could we be freed from these sins and experience eternal life in the presence of God.

After Lois shared the gospel with me in the quiet of our bedroom, a crystal-clear vision came to me. It is as clear today as it was on that July evening in 1973. I was on the road of life, approaching a "Y" in the road. I was free to choose which road to take. If I took the road to the right, I could continue my way, doing my thing, and our marriage would be over. But at the beginning of the road leading left, there was a road sign with two words on it: "Jesus Christ." I cannot tell you how, but it was absolutely clear to me that if I took that left fork in the road and accepted Jesus Christ as Lord and Savior, our marriage would be healed. It took me only a fraction of a second to make the most important decision I have ever made in my life. I did ask God's forgiveness for my sins and asked Jesus Christ to come into and take over my life!

No sirens or whistles went off immediately after making this life-changing decision, but when I awoke the next morning, there was no question that it was a different world! The world had not changed, but I had been changed. It was a clear, rather cool July morning. I got up early and rode my bicycle to work from our home on Sapsucker Woods Road in Ithaca. I felt that the weight of the world had been lifted from my shoulders; euphoria would describe my feelings. In fact, I literally cried all the way to the office. It is a wonder that I did not ride my bike over a bank or into a tree since I could not see where I was going through the tears.

My world has not been the same since. "He touched me and made me whole!" Watch and listen to this gospel song by the Gaither Vocal Band. —Bill Gaither and Gloria Gaither. He Touched Me. 1963. Gaither Vocal Band.

https://www.youtube.com/watch?v=5m--ptwd_iI.

He Touched Me
Shackled by a heavy burden,
'Neath a load of guilt and shame
Then the hand of Jesus touched me,
And now I am no longer the same.

He touched me, oh He touched me,
And oh, the joy that floods my soul!
Something happened and now I know,
He touched me and made me whole.

Since I met this blessed Savior,
Since He cleansed and made me whole,
I will never cease to praise Him,
I'll shout it while eternity rolls.

He touched me, oh He touched me,
And oh, the joy that floods my soul!
Something happened and now I know
He touched me and made me whole.

A couple of weeks after this life-changing experience, Lois asked me if I would go to church with her, and I agreed. Since I had no clue about any churches in the Ithaca area, I asked her what church she would like to attend. She wanted to go to a church she had heard about from several of her new friends called Bethel Grove Bible Church. We attended the worship service the next Sunday morning, and as I sat in the pew, I felt the clear presence of God within that sanctuary! It was a peace that I had not experienced before, and I wanted to continue in that peace. We have attended Bethel Grove regularly since 1973 and have been greatly blessed by the excellent teaching, preaching, and warm fellowship. The cornerstone of the church is engraved with, *For the Glory of God.*

My walk with the Lord has been a growing process as I gradually come to understand the fantastic yet undeserved grace of Jesus. I still fall short of the glory of the triune God (Father, Son, and Holy Spirit), but through this learning process I have gradually become more like the man He would have me be. I will never fully arrive at that point, short of Heaven, since I cannot earn redemption, and I understand this, for we all fall short of the glory of God. However, through His grace I have been forgiven of all my past, present, and future sins, and I look forward to eternal life with Him.

Each person comes to experience the saving grace of Christ in a different way. While I regret the thirty-seven years I spent without Christ in my life, I do treasure the dramatic "born-again," "Damascus Road" experience that He so graciously allowed me to experience. There are two verses from scripture that speak mightily about my experience. In Revelation 3:20, Jesus says, "Here I am! I stand at the door and knock. If anyone hears my voice and opens the door, I will come in and eat with him, and he with me." What a beautiful open door He provided for me! Secondly, in Second Corinthians 5:17, the Apostle Paul states, "Therefore, if anyone is in Christ, he is a new creation; the old has gone, the new has come." I am living proof that Christ is absolutely faithful to both promises.

The Narrow Gate

> Enter through the narrow gate. For wide is the gate and broad is the road that leads to destruction, and many enter through it. But small is the gate and narrow the road that leads to life, and only a few find it.
>
> —Matthew 7:13-14

This teaching by Jesus during his Sermon on the Mount illustrates the narrow gate, or narrow door, that we must pass through to develop a personal relationship with Jesus. There is also a narrow road we must follow after we pass through that narrow gate. He contrasts this with the wide gate and wide road that many pass through and travel without a personal relationship with Jesus—that wide road leads to destruction. As Josh Turner sings, *"Don't ride on that long black train."*—Josh Turner. Long Black Train. YouTube video, Gaither Studios. https://www.youtube.com/watch?v=ga-YvtC9JXw

The following are some thoughts on the narrow and wide gates, the narrow and wide roads, and the four choices we must make, presented in a sermon by Lead Pastor Eric Hause at Bethel Grove Bible Church. — Pastor Eric Hause. *Sermon, 11/4/2018.* Bethel Grove Bible Church. Ithaca, NY. http://bg.org/sundaymorning/sermons/

First, we have the choice of which gate, or door, we will pass through—the wide gate with all the tolerance and acceptance espoused by the world, or the narrow gate which is Jesus Christ. Enter is an active verb, and we must exercise it and enter through that narrow gate.

Second, we have the choice of which road we will take—the wide road or the narrow road. It is easy to pass through the wide gate and enter the well-traveled, wide road where everything is tolerated and accepted. The narrow road is not so easy. Even after we pass through that narrow gate, we still must traverse that narrow road. These two parallel roads are going in different directions, one moving toward God and the other moving away from God.

Third, we have the choice of companions with whom we interact as we traverse the road of life. That wide road has many persons, each doing what is right in his/her own eyes. The narrow road has fewer persons on it, but they provide accountability and fellowship to the follower of Jesus.

Fourth, we have the choice of the destiny at which we will ultimately arrive. The wide gate and wide road lead to destruction, while the narrow gate and road lead to eternal life.

Every person that comes to a personal relationship with Christ does so in a unique way. In my case, I had no interest in anything religious, was not seeking the Lord, had not been to a church in twenty years, and had never read the Bible. Yet the Lord in an instant gave me a vision that was so clear there was no doubt in my mind. I am eternally grateful that the Lord showed me that narrow gate or "narrow open door" and clearly showed me via a vision what the future would hold if I walked through that narrow door, repented of my sins, accepted Him as Lord and Savior, and traversed down that narrow road! He also made it crystal clear what would happen if I rejected Him and continued down the wide road that I was on. I shudder to think of what my life would be today, and what my family would be, if I had continued on that wide road that led to destruction—if I had continued to ride that "long black train!"

Why me, Lord?

I have often contemplated why the Lord grabbed hold of me and brought me gently to a saving grace. Why did He single me out when I had no interest in Him? What does He want me to do? What is my role as a Christian veterinarian within the veterinary profession, with my veterinary students, and with my fellow faculty members? What does He want me to do in my family, in my church, and in the community?

True, the Lord wants everyone to come to know Him and receive His saving grace and eternal life. And He has something for every one of these individuals to do using the spiritual gifts He has given that individual. But history has many examples where the Lord singled out certain persons to carry out great tasks that He has for them. The anti-Christian Zealot Paul was zapped on the road to Damascus, and he became the key spokesman for the Lord in the New Testament. The Lord took a "spiritually-dead," teenage, dairy-farm boy from North Carolina and transitioned him into a world preacher that led millions of individuals to a personal relationship with Jesus Christ. —Jerry Menges, *Young Billy Graham: 'In a Word I was Spiritually Dead.'* Decision. Nov. 2017:20-21

I certainly am not a "Paul" or a "Billy," but I was a spiritually-dead, former teenage dairy-farm boy that the Lord called to His service, opened doors for, and guided to heights and accomplishments within the veterinary profession that were unfathomable. All to His glory!

CHAPTER 3

God's Grace

> A man's steps are directed by the Lord.
> —Proverbs 20:24

In late September of 1979, I attended a committee meeting of the World Health Organization in Rome, Italy, in which the classification of a family of viruses was discussed. It was a Tuesday-to-Thursday noon meeting. I had a plane ticket to fly to Lyon, France, on Thursday afternoon to spend the weekend with a dear friend, Gilles Chappuis. Gilles had spent a few months in my laboratory at Cornell in the early 1970s to become familiar with the way to grow feline viruses in cell cultures for his company to begin producing vaccines for cats in Europe. Ever since he was at Cornell, he had been after me to visit him and his family in Lyon. This seemed like a perfect time to scoot up to Lyon from Rome, and I looked forward to this visit with great expectations.

On Wednesday afternoon the woman who coordinated travel for those attending the meeting checked with everyone to see if any changes needed to be made in their plane tickets. I recall that the strangest feeling came over me. I KNEW that I had to get home and not go to France. I did not know why, but it was crystal clear to me that I had to change my plans and return home to Ithaca. The travel coordinator changed my plane tickets and scheduled me to fly Friday from Rome to JFK airport in New York City, then on to Ithaca. With deep regret, I called my friend in Lyon and explained that I had to return home. I could not tell him why—I did not know why. With Thursday afternoon free, another committee member and I had a marvelous walking tour around Rome on a perfectly gorgeous afternoon.

Of course, this was before cell phones, text messages, and email—we just had the old-fashioned landline phones. When I arrived at JFK airport on Friday evening, I phoned Lois at home to alert her of my change in plans and that I would be home late that evening. It was then that she informed me that my mother had a heart attack on Wednesday—the same day that I had the epiphany that I must go directly home. My mother had been at camp in the Adirondacks with my sister Gladys when the attack occurred. Gladys drove her back to Greenfield, Massachusetts, and to the local hospital near Mom's home.

The next day (Saturday), Lois, our son Raymond, and I drove the five hours from Ithaca to Greenfield, Massachusetts, and went directly to the hospital. We found Mom very alert and sitting up in a chair watching a Boston Red Sox baseball game—she was a diehard Red Sox fan. We had a great visit, and of course she wanted to know all about my trip to Rome. We left her to rest and recuperate with a calm assurance that she was going to be all right.

From Greenfield, we drove the short way to Putney, Vermont, to spend the rest of the weekend with Lois's parents. We planned to visit Mom again Sunday afternoon on our way back to Ithaca. We had no more than arrived in Putney when I received a call informing me that, as the nurse was moving Mom from the chair back to her hospital bed, her damaged heart muscle ruptured, and she died immediately.

Mom had a strong faith in God, so she immediately transitioned from this world to a better place in the presence of Jesus. We were the last family members to visit her.

What is absolutely amazing to me is how the Lord got my attention at the moment Mom had her heart attack, and without letting me know why, made it crystal clear that I had to return home. In His amazing grace, He closed one door—my anticipated trip to France—and opened another to get me home in time to see my mother before she passed from this earth.

Gary Bolton

Dr. Gary Bolton was a fellow young faculty member at the Cornell College of Veterinary Medicine. He was a good friend and a truly knowledgeable, board-certified cardiologist in the Clinic. Gary was a gifted teacher, lecturer, diagnostician, and author. He was our go-to person for any cardiology questions that were presented to the Cornell Feline Health Center.

One day in the mid-1970s, not too long after I had accepted Christ as my savior, as I sat at my desk at work early in the morning, I received an astonishing directive from the Holy Spirit. Out of the blue, I was told to send Gary Bolton my testimony. I hesitated and questioned what Gary would think of me, since we had never discussed anything related to religion or the Lord. Again, I was instructed to send Gary my testimony.

So, reluctantly at first, I drafted a hand-written letter to Gary outlining in some detail my testimony, including how my accepting Jesus as my savior had saved my marriage. This was long before personal computers and instant email, so I sent the letter to Gary via campus mail.

A couple of days later, I received a note back from Gary. He thanked me for the letter, and then shared that he and his wife Jean were having problems with their marriage. A few discussions followed, and a few days later Gary accepted the Lord as his savior—Jean followed suit shortly thereafter. Praise the Lord! I am not an evangelist. Hopefully, I have planted a few seeds and perhaps watered a few seeds planted by others. But as far as I know, while I have shared my testimony numerous times when it seemed appropriate, this is the only time that the Lord used my testimony directly to knock on someone's door. Praise the Lord that Gary opened that door.

Gary, the legendary small animal clinician Dr. Robert Kirk, and I, plus a couple of other believing faculty members at the college, began meeting weekly for Bible study and prayer. These were special times.

One night I invited Gary to attend a Cornell men's hockey game with me. It was at that game that Gary shared that he had been diagnosed that afternoon with a malignant melanoma on his back. The next week at our faculty Bible study, Gary shared with the group his diagnosis and realization that the prognosis might not be good. He confided to the group that his future was secure because he had accepted Jesus as his savior, and he knew where he was going. But the thought of his two young children growing up without a father really bummed him out. He continued his teaching and clinical practice as if nothing were amiss.

One fall, a few years later, Gary and I went on a camping trip to Vermont. During our time together, Gary complained of severe headaches—he said that he would have to get his eyes checked and get new glasses. Shortly after returning from our trip, one of his residents in the clinic confided to me that each of his staff had independently begun checking up on each of his cases because he was missing diagnoses and appropriate treatment—very uncharacteristic for Gary. Eventual tests showed that it was not his eyes that were causing the headaches and other changes but a brain tumor. Brain surgery followed, but Gary died on February 10, 1982, at the age of thirty-nine, from complications following the surgery.

The veterinary students were traumatized by Dr. Bolton's death. During my regular Virology and Viral

Diseases lecture a day or two later, it was obvious that the students were in shock and disbelief. I made an offer to the class that anyone who wanted to share their feelings and questions could meet with me at a specified time and location the next day. To my surprise, about twenty-five of the eighty students in the class showed up for the discussion. A couple of the students were believers, but as far as I knew most were not. Open discussions occurred about faith, eternal life, and why bad things happen to really good people. I shared how Gary had accepted Jesus Christ as his savior, and how we could be confident that he was now in Heaven. I shared my testimony with the group as well—something that never could happen in a regular class setting at Cornell.

As I concluded my testimony, I was aware that a petite Jewish woman in the front row directly in front of me was very disturbed. She got up and hurriedly started for the door. I asked her to come back and offered an apology if I had offended her. She then shared with her classmates that she was going through a series of exceedingly difficult situations, and this was just too much for her to handle. An interesting and positive discussion followed with all the classmates. I was able to meet with her one-on-one several times, with open discussions about faith and the Gospel. She was interested, but I never knew whether she accepted the Lord as Savior.

At the students' request, we continued to meet weekly for several weeks. Twelve years later, at her ten-year class reunion, one of those students shared with me how important that discussion group was to her personally.

I thank the Lord for that open door to discuss faith with the veterinary students, and especially that He called Gary to become a believer! I look forward to seeing Gary one day in Heaven.

Evolution vs. Creation

During my eleven years of formal college education, evolution was repeatedly presented as fact. I never questioned it—there was no reason to question evolution. As a non-believer and several years before my amazing encounter with the Lord, I remember standing in front of a display case in an anatomy lab at the College of Veterinary Medicine at Cornell. As I compared the skeletons of several animal species that we deal with in veterinary medicine, I marveled at the similarity of the skeletons. Basically, all mammals have seven cervical (neck) vertebrae—horse, cow, pig, goat, dog, cat, mouse, giraffe. This was confirmation to me of evolution, and I marveled at how each specie had evolved from one to another over the millions of years. I even recall using this argument of the similarities of animal skeletons as proof of evolution in a discussion with two Mormon missionaries that stopped at our house one evening. I am sure I did not convince them, but in my mind the discussion was over.

At age thirty-seven, shortly after I had received a promotion to associate professor with tenure in the Microbiology Department at the College of Veterinary

Medicine, the Lord got hold of me, and literally overnight my world completely changed: I accepted the Lord as my Savior.

I had not been to church in twenty years and had never read the Bible. I was a brand-new baby, born-again Christian. Suddenly, I was confronted with this thing called "creation." I did not know how to handle it, since it was completely contrary to everything I had been taught in all the science courses that I had taken. I felt myself being pulled in two different directions. The Lord quietly spoke to me, saying, "Fred, don't worry about creation now, in time you will understand." So, I did not think about creation or evolution for about three years. Then, as I got somewhat grounded in my faith, I was able to go back and look at creation vs. evolution and look at the evidence for each. I am so thankful that the Lord, in His marvelous grace, gave me time to become grounded—in essence, He temporarily closed the door on evolution vs. creation. Otherwise, who knows, this baby Christian may have turned away from his new faith.

As I reflected on the marvelous construction of the human and animal bodies, taking a completely new approach to the evidence before me, it became obvious to me that this fantastic machine called the "body" did not just happen by chance mutations over millions of years. There had to be a designer. Each organ or system in the body has a specific function, and there are built-in checks and balances to allow the organ or system to function at just the right degree. Take the immune system, for example. When a cat is infected with a virus, certain cells within the cat's body are able to react to that virus, or a specific portion of that virus, and produce antibodies that neutralize the virus and make the cat immune to that virus in the future. In the last fifty years, tremendous advances have been made to better understand the immune system and how it works. We now know that it is an extraordinarily complex system, with all kinds of immune-related entities taking part in the immune response. It is a magnificent and awe-inspiring system when one really looks at what is going on. That all happened by chance? I do not think so. The more scientists learn about specific systems, the more convincing it is that these systems just did not happen by chance. To God be the glory!

Knowledge to Wisdom

Growing up on a farm during the Great Depression and World War II, I was "home-schooled" at my dad and mom's sides, receiving a lot of common-sense knowledge relating to work, living, and survival in difficult times. This included valuable information related to animals (cattle, dogs, cats, chickens, rabbits, pheasants) and basic farm skills related to hard work, gardening, understanding machinery, haying, handling crops, apple production, producing maple syrup, logging, and carpentry. From my dad and two older brothers, I also received excellent training in fishing, hunting, baseball, and basketball. Sprinkled into this "home-schooling" were gems of information about people, interacting with people, and respecting people, animals, and nature.

Twelve years of elementary and high school in a small rural school provided my basic formal education. Following graduation from high school, eleven of the next fourteen years, including eight of the first eleven years of marriage, were spent as a full-time college student. My higher educational training had a concentration on biology and science, veterinary medicine, and virology and immunology. I was a professional student—some say I was just a slow learner. This college education resulted in three degrees: BS, DVM, and PhD. To survive all this college training, I needed to accumulate a great deal of knowledge in many areas. With all this knowledge, my early successes in research as a faculty member at the College of Veterinary Medicine, and numerous opportunities to speak to veterinarians at meetings across the country, it became easy to begin thinking about all the great things I had accomplished. Fortunately, the Lord graciously knocked that pedestal I had climbed upon completely out from under me!

Five years after completing my PhD, and shortly after being promoted to associate professor with tenure in 1973, the Lord dramatically opened the most significant door of my life. He led me into a personal relationship with Him, gave me a new heart, and my life was changed forever!

What followed was a gradual realization over forty-five-plus years that all this common sense and knowledge I had accumulated needed to be seasoned with wisdom and a great dose of humility. This process ebbed and flowed, with two steps forward, and one step backward, and it is still being worked out to this day. I am still a work in progress.

Instead of throwing the door to wisdom wide open, the Lord gradually opened the door a crack at a time to let me see one sliver of wisdom at a time, thus allowing me to apply that sliver of wisdom to my life. As a result, over time I learned to not take myself or my accomplishments too seriously, and to acknowledge wholeheartedly that anything that this naive farm kid was able to accomplish was not by my abilities alone, but through the leading, gracious gifts, and open doors provided by Jesus Christ. To God be the glory!

The biblical book of Proverbs has been called the "Book of Wisdom." Proverbs, plus some verses in Psalms, shed light on the grace of the Lord, unfolding the powerful aspects of wisdom, and explicitly pointing out the positive future of those that acquire wisdom and the negative future for those that do not acquire wisdom. Here are some powerful verses from the NIV Bible. (Note: "fear" denotes being in awe of, or having great respect for, rather than being afraid of the Lord.)

> The fear of the Lord is the beginning of wisdom; all who follow his precepts have good understanding. To him belongs eternal praise —Psalm 111:10

> The fear of the Lord is the beginning of knowledge, but fools [denotes ones who are morally deficient] despise wisdom and discipline. —Proverbs 1:7

1My son, if you accept my words and store up my commands within you, 2turning your ear to wisdom and applying your heart to understanding, 3and if you call out for insight and cry aloud for understanding, 4and if you look for it as for silver and search for it as for hidden treasure, 5then you will understand the fear of the Lord and find the knowledge of God. 6For the Lord gives wisdom, and from his mouth come knowledge and understanding. —Proverbs 2:1-6

12Wisdom will save you from the ways of wicked men . . .. 20Thus, you will walk in the ways of good men and keep to the paths of the righteous. —Proverbs 2:12, 20

5Trust in the Lord with all your heart and lean not on your own understanding; 6in all your ways acknowledge him, and he will make your paths straight. —Proverbs 3:5-6

13Blessed is the man who finds wisdom, the man who gains understanding, 14for she is more profitable than silver and yields better returns than gold. 15She is more precious than rubies; nothing you desire can compare with her. —Proverbs 3:13-15

5Get wisdom, get understanding; do not forget my words or swerve from them. 6Do

not forsake wisdom, and she will protect you; love her, and she will watch over you. 7Wisdom is supreme; therefore, get wisdom. Though it cost all you have, get understanding. 8Esteem her, and she will exalt you; embrace her, and she will honor you.
—Proverbs 4:5-8

Above all else, guard your heart, for it is the wellspring of life. —Proverbs 4:23

Peace that Surpasses All Understanding

On several occasions, when significant health issues or other stressful situations have occurred in my or my wife's life, I have been amazed at the peace that the Lord has bestowed upon Lois and me. His amazing grace and peace have been wonderful. The extensive band of prayer warrior friends within our church and around the country certainly contribute to that peace we have felt.

In 1998, I experienced a mild heart attack early one Friday morning. Over the next ten days, there were many situations and times when I could have been really stressed out. However, throughout this whole ordeal, the Lord gave me a wonderful peace about the whole thing—that peace that surpasses all understanding.

He even allowed me to see a few humorous things along the way. First, both of my parents had died from a heart attack years before, so I was a prime suspect to have a severe heart attack. There was the stay in our local hospital over the weekend, then a forty-mile transport via ambulance to Robert Packer Hospital in Sayre, PA, then the cardiac catheterization on Monday which showed the ten lesions partially blocking my cardiac arteries. The cardiologist explained that the size of the arteries involved, and the location of the lesions prevented the use of stints, so bypass surgery was required. There were plenty of possible stress points for worry.

To my question to my cardiologist of when I should have the surgery, he responded abruptly, "I'd wait a week!" Realizing how odd this must have come across to me, he laughed and responded, "The person that should do the surgery is on vacation and will be back next Monday." This was mid-July, and I found out later that there was a new heart surgeon that started July 1, and he was having a few stressful situations himself. So, I was blessed that the cardiologist arranged to have the wonderful and remarkably successful heart surgeon, Dr. Reitknecht, do the surgery a week later.

After the pre-surgery routine the day before the scheduled surgery, Lois was driving me home when I suddenly burst out laughing. Then I shared with Lois what I found funny. I said, "The Lord sure has a sense of humor. In 1973, at my dramatic conversion, He gave me a new heart, and tomorrow, twenty-five years later *to the day*, He is going to give me some new plumbing for that heart!"

The quadruple bypass surgery went well. After

the usual rehab period of about six months, I was back to playing senior basketball with my buddies.

On several occasions I, and another member, have shared with the Men's Bible study and prayer group the amazing peace that surpasses all understanding that both of us experienced going into heart surgery with Dr. Reitknecht.

In the spring of 2010, Lois was diagnosed with stage 3 ovarian cancer. Now that is a diagnosis that can result in a lot of stress and worry! But again, the Lord provided us with a great deal of peace as we traveled along this journey—all the tests, the surgery, six months of chemotherapy, and several years of follow-up exams and tests. Ten years down the road, she is cancer-free. Praise the Lord! It certainly was not a journey that we would have chosen, but we experienced many blessings and God's grace along the way.

As we drove to Rochester, New York, the day before her surgery, we were listening to a Gaither Vocal Band CD. The song that came on had the following lyrics: *"Because He lives, I can face tomorrow. Because He lives, all fear is gone. Because I know He holds the future, and life is worth the living just because He lives."* —Bill and Gloria Gaither. Because He lives. Gaither Vocal Band. https://www.youtube.com/watch?v=2Oz_caE8oQE

We grabbed hold of that song, and the Lord used it to give us the peace and comfort we needed as we traveled that long cancer journey.

Lois's book of LOISisms and one-liners was

published two weeks after her surgery. We had a lot of fun sharing this book with Lois's fellow chemo patients during the many months of her chemo. —Lois E. Scott, Caleb F. Scott, Fred W. Scott. *If You Want to Soar with Eagles, Don't Hang Out with Turkeys: Gems for Christian Living.* iUniverse, 2010

CHAPTER 4

The Road to Veterinary Medicine

Career Decision

It was during my junior year of high school (fall 1952) that I went through the process of selecting a potential career and a college in which to be trained for that career. Like many boys growing up in New England, I dreamt of playing baseball for the Boston Red Sox. As reality set in, however, it became apparent I better pursue another career. One option was to stay on the family farm and work with my dad and brother, Bud. I enjoyed farm life in a small community, and I liked animals. It would be the easy option to just slide into this situation after high school, but for whatever reason, this did not seem to be the appropriate career for me. Was the Lord stepping in to guide me on to the career that He had chosen for me? Was this one of several closed doors I would encounter?

After considerable thought about possible options, I decided to pursue veterinary medicine as a career. As I recall, my thought process went something like the following: (1) I like animals and want to work with cattle (2) I do not want to live in a big city but rather remain in a rural setting (3) I am not interested in making a lot of money, but I want to earn enough money so that I can buy a new shotgun if I want. It seemed that a career as a rural veterinarian working with dairy cattle would meet all three of these criteria.

I knew only one veterinarian at the time—Dr. Charles Streeter, who did the veterinary work for the cattle on the home farm. I reasoned that I would follow his example. This was the only part of veterinary medicine that I was aware of at the time. I did not have a clue as to what the Lord had in store for me regarding this fabulous profession called veterinary medicine, nor was I aware of the doors that He would open in the future or the ways He would lead me to unbelievable heights.

Funny how small, insignificant thoughts can sometimes affect your decisions about your future. Why did the idea of buying a shotgun enter my career decision? Because we grew up on a small farm during the Great Depression and World War II, other than playing basketball and baseball, hunting and fishing were the prime areas of recreation for my dad, my two older brothers, and myself. There was no extra money for non-essentials. I started hunting on the family farm when I was ten years old. As a young teenager, I worked hard all summer nailing up apple boxes for neighboring farms in order to purchase, for twenty-eight dollars, an inexpensive Mossberg 3-shot Bolt Action 20-gauge shotgun. Bud always went deer hunting each fall with our veterinarian Dr. Streeter and his wife. His hunting stories inevitably included mention of the beautiful Browning semi-automatic shotguns that Dr. Streeter and his wife had. Hence the connection of money and a shotgun that entered my career decision.

When I told my mother that I wanted to become a veterinarian, she replied in her direct, to-the-point way, "Why don't you become a real doctor?" I laughed and replied that I wanted to work on animals, not people. That was the last time she questioned my career decision, and from then on, Mom and Dad were fully supportive of my career decision.

Undergraduate Pre-Veterinary Training

For undergraduate college, only one application was submitted—to the University of Massachusetts in Amherst. This seemed to be the only avenue open to me since UMass was a state university, and the tuition was very modest for Massachusetts residents. I did not have any financial resources, and my parents were not able to pay for tuition, room, and board, so I would have to work my way through college. Thankfully, I was accepted as a pre-veterinary student with a double major in zoology and chemistry—the first of many open doors on the road to veterinary medicine!

In September 1954, I entered UMass and roomed with Al Kendrick from Ashfield, a classmate for twelve years at Sanderson Academy. Most freshmen at UMass had classes on Saturday, but for some reason, I did not. Therefore, every Friday night I would return home for a clean set of clothes and restock on goodies from the farm. This also kept the cost down, as I did not have to buy meals on the weekends. My future wife, Lois, had started working in Springfield, Massachusetts, that summer, so she took my car (a 1940 Oldsmobile) and dropped me off at college Sunday evening, then picked me up Friday evening for the twenty-five-mile ride home.

At UMass, I joined the agricultural fraternity, Alpha Gamma Rho, the same fraternity that my dad belonged to when he was a student there from 1916-1920. Two of my fraternity brothers were also pre-vet majors, and they were helpful in guiding me in my required classes and the application process.

Since I had played basketball and baseball in high school, it was natural to consider doing the same in college. A major dose of reality set in when I tried out for the freshman basketball team and I was cut after the second practice. Baseball was slightly more successful, as I made the freshman team as the fourth-string catcher. Obviously, I did not see playing time from that position. I did make the varsity baseball team my second and third years as a utility infielder, but again I was only warming the bench. During my senior year, I had a full academic schedule with several afternoon science labs, and it was obvious I was not going to make the starting lineup, so I dropped baseball. It was fun, however, attending the practices and the games, and interacting with a great bunch of guys for three years.

In order to qualify to submit an application to veterinary college, I took all the courses that were offered that were either required or recommended for admission to the two veterinary colleges that would accept my application—Cornell University and the University of Pennsylvania in Philadelphia. There was not a college of veterinary medicine in New England. At this time in the 1950s, the other fifteen US veterinary colleges restricted their applicant pools to state residents or to residents of states with which that college had a contract to accept a limited number of students. While only two years of pre-veterinary college were required for admission to veterinary college most applicants from out-of-state did not apply until the fall of their senior years. By all accounts, it was a daunting task to gain admission to a veterinary college from Massachusetts in the 1950s. All pre-vet majors were advised to have an alternate career plan.

Academically, I did okay at UMass, but by no means did I sail through the curriculum—I made the Dean's List in only one of eight semesters. Science and math were okay, but languages and liberal arts classes were not my strong suits. Although this was before grade inflation hit US colleges, my academic credentials were not a strong point in my applications to veterinary college. Was I up against a closed door in my pursuit of veterinary medicine? Would I have to go to Plan B? Fortunately, I had a strong farm background and a keen interest in large animal veterinary practice, both of which were of great importance to admission to veterinary colleges in the 1950s.

My advisor was clear. He would give me a good recommendation, but he seriously doubted I would ever be accepted at a veterinary college—rarely was anyone from Massachusetts accepted at any veterinary college. It was evident to me that the road ahead to gain admission to a veterinary college at either Cornell University or the University of Pennsylvania was going to be difficult, and that I very well could be denied admission like so many previous applicants from Massachusetts.

However, in the fall of my senior year at UMass, I proceeded to fill out and submit applications for admission to both the New York State College of Veterinary Medicine at Cornell (as it was known then), and to the College of Veterinary Medicine at the University of Pennsylvania. Although I did not realize it at the time, the rest was in the hands of the Lord.

College of Veterinary Medicine

In due time during the winter of 1958, I received letters from both Cornell and the University of Pennsylvania. The letter from Cornell granted me an interview in early March 1958. My wife Lois and I drove to Ithaca, and I checked in at the dean's office at the specified time. I was a nervous wreck at that point—the whole future rested on this interview, or so I thought. The dean's secretary graciously stopped what she was doing and began chatting with me. Boy was that helpful to calm me down.

I was called across the hall to the interview, which was chaired by the eminent Dean Walter Hagan; two faculty members rounded out the interview committee. I recall a couple of the questions Dean Hagan asked me sixty years ago as clear as if they had been asked yesterday. After introductions and a few niceties, he started out by asking, "I see that you are married. How are going to pay for four years of veterinary college?" Nothing like getting right to the point. I explained that Lois was currently employed at UMass, and she planned to continue to work and support our family while I was in veterinary college. I would work at whatever jobs were available as the limited time allowed.

Later, Dean Hagan stated, "I see you have experience with draft horses. What is the *crupper* of the harness?" I had experience with a wonderful old draft horse skidding logs, but I had never learned all the names of the straps that make up the harness. A few days before the interview, I was looking up something in the dictionary, and a sketch of a horse and harness with the parts of the harness named caught my eye. I recall thinking, *that would be a good question to ask in my upcoming interview.* I stopped and spent a few minutes going over the names of the parts of the harness. So, I was able to answer Dean Hagan's question that the crupper was the strap that went around the rear of the horse under the tail. Was that just coincidence that I stopped and studied that illustration only a few days before the interview? Or was a higher power guiding me that day, shedding light on the open door to come?

A week after the interview I received my acceptance to the Class of 1962 at the New York State College of Veterinary Medicine at Cornell. Wow! I was ecstatic! What an open door to a fabulous career opportunity in veterinary medicine!

> 7What he opens, no one can shut; and what he shuts, no one can open. 8I know your deeds. See, I have placed before you an open door that no one can shut.
>
> — Revelation 3:7-8.

Several years later, when I was chairman of the admissions committee at Cornell, I was reviewing the number of applicants per year to the college. Usually, there were up to one thousand applicants each year for sixty to eighty spots in the class—extremely competitive. The year that I applied had by far the fewest number of applicants for any year since World War II. That helped explain just how fortunate and blessed I was to be granted one of the twenty spots reserved for non-New York State applicants in the Class of 1962!

The room where my admissions interview occurred eventually became known as the Hagan Room, with a large portrait of Dean Hagan on the wall. During the many years I was a faculty member at the college, every time I entered that room and saw the portrait of Dean Hagan, I had a flashback to my admissions interview so many years before.

Before my interview and acceptance at Cornell, I received a letter from the admissions office at the University of Pennsylvania that stated my application to the veterinary college was denied. Seems someone from the Pennsylvania Department of Education had denied my application because I had not graduated from an accredited high school. What? I had four years of college grades, but I was being dinged for my high school.

The next day I stopped at the registrar's office at UMass and showed him the letter. He exploded. He said that Sanderson Academy, my high school, was fully accredited by the New England Association of Schools and Colleges, and that was the only accrediting board in New England. He called in his secretary, had me take a seat, and proceeded to dictate a scathing letter in reply. A few days later, I received notification from admissions at Penn that I had a scheduled interview. By that time, I had my acceptance at Cornell, which was my first choice, so I respectfully declined the interview and withdrew my application to Penn.

My four years at Cornell as a veterinary student were incredibly special. They were a tremendous amount of work, but the amazing fields of biology and medicine opened up to me. I was taught by one of the best, if not the best, faculty in veterinary medicine at the time. Each one was a giant in his or her own field! It was a real privilege and blessing to be tutored by such an amazing group of experts. Isaac Newton in 1676 expressed my sentiment and thankfulness for my professors at the CVM: "If I have seen further, it is by standing on the shoulders of giants."

The CVM had moved from the "old" facilities in the central campus to the "new" facilities at the east end of Tower Road one year before our class enrolled. Sixty students started the four-year veterinary program in September 1958, and fifty-six graduated with a Doctor of Veterinary Medicine (DVM) degree in May 1962. Only one student failed out of the program, and a few transferred to medical school after one or two years.

The class schedule was basically 8:00 a.m. to 5:00 p.m. each day, with a break for lunch, plus Saturday morning classes. The entire day was filled with classes and labs, all of which everyone was required to take. There were no elective courses.

The first year consisted of a large portion of anatomy for both semesters, five days a week, with an extensive prelim exam on Monday morning each week. The anatomy of the dog was studied during the fall semester, then the anatomies of the horse, cow, sheep, and chicken were studied during the spring semester. The anatomy professors were Drs. Malcolm Miller and Howard Evans along with various graduate assistants. Other topics included physiology, taught by Dr. Dukes; histology; and poisonous plants. There was a brand new, never used histology lab right next to the anatomy lab. However, since the college had a ten-year teaching agreement with the zoology faculty down campus, we got the privilege of taking the twenty-minute walk down campus each day to take the histology class in the zoology building, taught by the same faculty that taught the pre-med students.

A genuine fear of failure during the first semester drove me to study as hard as possible. I recall starting to study for the Monday anatomy prelim on Friday evening each week, continuing Saturday evening, and again all-day Sunday. A brief respite from studying on Saturday afternoon was the only time to enjoy my wife and young son Duane. After the first semester, I realized that I could survive veterinary college without having to panic—I just had to keep up with the vast amount of material presented each day and not get behind. If you got behind, there was no way to catch up.

The second-year veterinary curriculum included topics such as pathology (taught by Drs. Peter Olafson and John King), bacteriology and virology (taught by Drs. Dorsey Bruner and Leland Carmichael), public health (taught by Dr. Peter Olafson), infectious diseases (taught by Dean George Poppensiek), and parasitology (taught by Dr. Donald Baker and an assistant).

The third-year veterinary curriculum moved into clinical and surgical medicine. Large animal medicine was a major emphasis and was taught by Dr. Francis Fox. Small animal medicine was usually taught by Dr. Robert Kirk, but that year he was on sabbatical leave, so he had a recent graduate with one year of general practice experience teach the course using Dr. Kirk's lecture notes. This was the one example where one of the "giants" on the faculty was missed by our class. Large animal surgery was taught by Dr. Gordon Danks, and small animal surgery, including detailed training in sterile surgical techniques, was taught by Dr. Ellis Leonard. Obstetrics was taught by Dr. Steve Roberts. Applied anatomy was taught by Drs. Robert Habel and Alexander (Sandy) deLahunta. Avian diseases were taught by Dr. P. P. Levine.

The senior year of the veterinary curriculum was devoted primarily to clinics, with rotations through (1) the large animal clinic, (2) the small animal clinic, (3) the ambulatory clinic where local farms were visited, and (4) pathology. One lecture on large animal medicine, taught by Dr. Myron Fincher, started each day.

Each senior class member was required to select a clinical case, work up the case, write up a report, and present a seminar to the CVM. The case I selected was skin tuberculosis in cattle. The organism that causes this infection is related to the organism that causes bovine tuberculosis (TB) and thus often causes cattle to react "positive" to the TB test.

Each veterinary class develops its own personality. Ours was a great class. We had a lot of fun along with working hard, and we worked together to help each other out rather than competing. Class reunions are always fun, with a lot of sharing about the good old times while at the CVM.

Many of my classmates got married either before attending Cornell or during the four years. There was a wonderful "vet wives" group that was special to Lois as they gathered and supported each other. At the end of the four years, the vet wives held a "graduation," and the seniors received a "PHT" degree for "Putting Hubby Through." Boy, did they ever support us as we were required to spend so much time and energy in the classrooms, labs, library, and clinics.

With all the stress and time commitment we were under, not all the marriages survived the four years.

In the first semester, my anatomy lab partner came back from Christmas vacation a zombie. I asked him what was the matter, and he said his wife left him after Christmas. His wife's parents had visited over the holiday, and his wife and young daughter went home with her parents, never to return. He was at the college studying, and when he got home that day all he found was a note and a cleaned-out house. Somehow, he managed to survive finals that first semester, then was able to regroup and complete the four years.

My veterinary class initially consisted of fifty-eight men and two women. For many years, only one, two, or three women were admitted in each class. This "token" admission is a sad part of earlier veterinary medicine, the false belief that the profession was a man's profession, restricted primarily to large animal medicine. Fortunately, that view has completely changed, and veterinary classes now are usually 75-85% women, with acceptance based on the merits of the applicant and closely mirroring the percentage of men and women applicants.

CHAPTER 5

Veterinary Medicine
~
The Early Years

The Lord bestowed many blessings upon me as a veterinarian. To my great amazement, He opened doors for me that I did not know were there, and He also closed a few doors that I thought were open for me, but in reality, were not meant to be. Here is my story of fifty-seven years in veterinary medicine.

Lois and I decided we would prefer to return to New England after veterinary college if I was fortunate enough to obtain a position there in a veterinary practice. I wanted to gain experience working in a veterinary practice before I set up my own dairy cattle practice, preferably in western Massachusetts. During my senior year, I began contacting veterinary practices that I knew about, especially in western Massachusetts and Connecticut. A graduate student in pathology who had recently returned to Cornell for graduate training contacted me and said the veterinarian that he had worked for in Fair Haven, Vermont, was looking to hire a new graduate veterinarian for their relatively new practice in Rutland, Vermont.

During Christmas break, Lois and I set out to visit veterinary clinics to see if they might have an opening for a new graduate and to visit the Rutland Veterinary Clinic. (I even visited in person a veterinarian in Connecticut who was in bed with the mumps.) None of the clinics we visited were looking to hire a new veterinarian. So, it was on to Rutland for my pre-arranged visit.

Rutland Veterinary Clinic

The Rutland Veterinary Clinic had been established by two veterinarians the year before. Dr. Charles Hults had practiced solo in a predominately large animal practice for twenty-five years in West Rutland, and Dr. Don Icken had practiced in Fair Haven for fifteen years. Rutland Veterinary Clinic was a mixed animal practice, about 50% large animal and 50% small animal. The practice had grown, and they needed to add a third veterinarian. They offered me a job, and after some negotiations about salary, Lois and I decided we would make Rutland our new home.

First, there were a few things I had to take care of: finish Senior year of veterinary college, take state boards, and move. Senior year was special, and all fifty-six classmates graduated. State boards were a different story.

A single national board for veterinary medicine was just on the horizon and examining boards for each state were still administering their own exams. New York boards consisted of five days of written and oral practical exams. Your knowledge in every field of veterinary medicine was thoroughly tested. I recall the New York boards as being tough but fair. Massachusetts boards had a shorter written exam period but also had their own peculiarities. They had a reputation for being a bit political depending upon what veterinary practice you were going to work at. On top of that, the new national boards were being introduced, so the Massachusetts board of veterinary examiners decided it would examine us in each topic—anatomy, biochemistry, pathology, etc.—with both their own exam and the national board exam.

Vermont boards, by contrast, were a breeze and a pleasure to take. The board exam was administered in the Senate Chambers at the state capitol in Montpelier. The entire written exam consisted of ten questions. Each was a specific case you might encounter in practice, and you were asked how you would handle each case. Most everyone taking the exam was done in less than two hours, and we heard the results within just a few days. One person taking the Vermont boards was going to work for his father-in-law in his veterinary practice, but his father-in-law had died a few weeks before, so he was taking over the practice and needed his Vermont license ASAP. The examining board graded his exam as he waited, and he had his license the same day as the exam. Now, that is using common sense to solve a difficult problem. Anyway, I passed the state boards for all three states.

A second-year veterinary student that I had worked with in the drug room of the ambulatory clinic had an old cattle truck, and he offered to move us to

Vermont. He cleaned up the old truck, and we loaded our meager belongings and headed to Vermont to begin this fabulous career in veterinary medicine.

I recall my first farm call driving to a Vermont farm solo to treat a young bull that was off feed. There was a bit of trepidation, and I had the question in my mind of whether I was ready to tackle this profession. Everything worked out all right, so I was off and running.

In New England, farmers often refer to veterinarians as "vetinary" or "vetinarian." On my first day at the clinic, I rode around to the farms with Dr. Hults, and he introduced me to some of the farmers. At one small farm of about twenty beautiful Holstein cows, the elderly farmer welcomed me and added, "I'll reserve judgment on what kind of a vetinary you are until I see the results. If you do a good job, I'll spread the word." He was a great guy and a great farmer who took excellent care of his cows. What a pleasure to work for him. I knew I could not pull any wool over his eyes, but I could be brutally honest with him. I was not afraid to say *I do not know*, and he was willing to accept that. Every case I treated on the farm, including a couple of extremely sick cows, responded beautifully to the treatment. That is a tribute to the way he kept the cows, not to any extraordinary treatment I was able to give.

Late one afternoon, an excellent first calf heifer at that farm was down and out with a severe intestinal disorder. Rapid laboratory diagnostic tests were not available, so the treatment had to be based on the clinical exam and the clinical signs she was showing. The problem—I could not figure out what was causing this severe disease. I told the farmer that I did not know what was causing the severe disease, but that I would treat her as hard as I could for everything that I could see clinically, and I would be back first thing in the morning to recheck her. I was sure she would not make it through the night. The next morning right after I got to the clinic, the farmer called and said, "Doc, don't bother to come look at that sick cow." My heart sank—I knew she had died. He then started to laugh and exuberantly stated, "She is up, eating, and looking fine."

There were many marginal farms in the hills around Rutland at that time, and not all cases responded like those on this special farm.

Shortly after I started working at the Rutland Veterinary Clinic, I was the only person in the clinic one noon hour. A woman and her spit-fire teenage daughter stopped in the clinic and asked for Dr. Icken. I responded, "He is not here, but I'm Dr. Scott. Can I help you?" The teenage gal looked me straight in the eye, made her evaluation of me, and emphatically stated, "You ain't no vetinary! You ain't going to touch my horse!" It struck me as hilarious, and I just burst out laughing. That family was a dead ringer for the Beverly Hillbillies, but over time I got to know them, and several times I treated their menagerie of animals.

One day I returned to the clinic from farm calls. Dr. Icken was terribly busy with small animal cases, and he asked if I would spay a cat. As I removed my boots and coveralls and scrubbed up for surgery, Dr. Icken anesthetized the cat, and the vet tech clipped, prepped, and draped the cat. When I walked into the surgery room, the very long-haired cat that I had never seen before—and even now could only see its head—was fully draped and ready for surgery. I made the small abdominal incision and inserted the spay hook into the incision to catch and extract the uterus. After three to four tries without success, I told the vet tech, "Jim, check under the tail." Jim picked up the edge of the surgical drape and quietly stated, "Doc, the 'ovaries' are under the tail." So, just like that, I became a member of the illustrious society of V.W.H.S.T.C. (Veterinarians Who Have Spayed Tomcats). It turned out the owner was someone that Lois and I square danced with, so I took a fair amount of razzing for "spaying" his tomcat, even though he'd brought the cat to the clinic to be "spayed."

It was a great experience at the Rutland Veterinary Clinic, and Lois and I look back at our time in Rutland with many fond memories. Drs. Hults and Icken were great to work for, they were great teachers, and the clinic was state-of-the-art for the early 1960s. The experience gave me great exposure to both large and small animal medicine. This turned out to be a wonderful open door to veterinary practice. I could not have found a better clinic in which to work and learn the ins and outs of veterinary practice. Thank you, Lord, for opening this special door!

We made many friends, and we felt our roots were

growing deeper in Rutland. Lois and I joined a square dance club, and I play on a slow-pitch softball team that won the Vermont state championship and placed third in New England. At the time, I thought perhaps this was where I would spend the rest of my veterinary career. I could easily eventually become a partner in this very promising clinic and perhaps the owner in future years. However, the Lord had other plans.

While in Rutland, I received a draft notice from the US Army Veterinary Corps. In the early 1960s, as the need for veterinarians arose to care for military animals, public health, food inspection, and research, each state had a quota of one or more veterinarians to be drafted to fill the Veterinary Corps. My name came up from Massachusetts, my home state. At UMass, it was compulsory for men who had not been in the service to take two years of ROTC. I took the two years in the Air Force ROTC and had the option to continue for the final two years and receive a commission and serve the required years of active duty. I declined because I wanted to move straight to veterinary college. I did not know at the time that it would have been possible to continue in ROTC and defer active duty until after finishing veterinary college. Some of my veterinary classmates had done that, and it was financially beneficial for them as well. As a student, I had a student deferment for my last two years at UMass, and for my four years of veterinary college. In the last five of those student years I was married.

So, I reported to Greenfield, Massachusetts, to join the other potential draftees for a bus trip to Springfield, where we were to get our physicals and sit for the pre-induction tests. As I recall, there was one other professional, and the rest were regular draftees. The two of us were separated and went through the physical and testing period in record time. I was listed as 1A and told to go home and that the Veterinary Corps would contact me when I was needed. So, I returned to Rutland and figured my time in private practice would be in for a hiatus of a couple of years. I never heard from the draft bureau or the Veterinary Corps, never got inducted, and was not even contacted to be informed that they no longer wanted me. I never asked. Perhaps I am still classified as 1A. From other sources, I learned that the Veterinary Corp had changed its practice, dropped the veterinary draft, and went to a total volunteer corps. Another closed door.

Potential Free Large Animal Practice

During my second year at Rutland (1963-64), a veterinarian from Greenfield, Massachusetts, contacted me with an unbelievable offer. He wanted to transition from a mixed large and small animal practice to just a small animal practice, a common occurrence for older veterinarians. He offered to GIVE me his large animal practice. He was concerned about his large animal clients, and he wanted someone to take over providing good veterinary care. I could use his office and two-way radio until I got my own place. This was a dream come true! This is what I had been working toward for more than ten years, and now it was being dumped in my lap. I would have my own large animal practice in western Massachusetts—an established practice that I did not have to pay for. I have never heard of another situation like this before, or since, except when it is a family situation. I was on cloud nine. What a tremendous open door!

In preliminary planning, I figured I would need only $1,500 to buy a used practice car and a few pieces of equipment. I had no money saved up at that time, so I went to the bank that had carried the mortgage on my father's farm to get a loan. After I shared the situation with the banker and made my request for $1,500, he said the bank would grant the loan if I could get an area veterinarian to co-sign the loan. That blew me away, and I replied, "If you don't think it is worth the risk for fifteen hundred dollars to start a new veterinary practice in the area, perhaps I need to think about it more."

I went home and shared this experience with Lois. Her response was that I would have a difficult time in practice in my hometown area because I would not be able to charge family and friends what I should to make a go of the practice. She knew me better than I knew myself, and she was absolutely right. She had not shared that with me before, and in retrospect, the Lord used her wise council, and that banker, to slam shut what I had thought was an unbelievable open door.

What followed next was an interesting exercise in "What now?" I still was not a believer, and of course, I did not see His guidance. However, unbeknownst to me, He was guiding me with more open and closed doors. With the door of my own large animal practice closed, what was my next step? Of course, I could stay at the Rutland Veterinary Clinic; it was a growing practice and had a very promising future. However, something was stirring in me that alerted me of my need to search elsewhere. I began visiting other clinics on my off days and had a couple of interesting opportunities, including joining a five-veterinarian practice in Cortland, New York. This practice had been highlighted during my large animal medicine courses by Dr. Fox as the ideal practice, and I had spent one day during vet school riding with the senior partner. I also thought some about an academic career in teaching and research, although I had not had any experience in these areas.

Legendary Dr. Fox, Sage Advice, and a Wonderful Open Door

So, I made a visit to Cornell to seek council from the legendary Dr. Francis Fox, whom I had worked for during the last three years as a veterinary student. In a brief visit of not more than fifteen minutes, he gave me better advice than I had ever received before or since. He closed a few doors for me and opened a new door that I had no clue existed. When I told him about my job offer at the Cortland practice, his reply was, "If they pay you enough to make it worth your while, fine, but don't go in there with a low salary and the promise to become a partner in a year. That practice may not be in existence in a year." Wow! He knew that practice and that it was about to implode with the five veterinarians going their separate ways. He kept me from a bad situation that I had not been aware of.

Next, he gave some good advice about a couple of academic fields I expressed possible interest in. His advice made sense, and I did not pursue them further. I did express a possible interest in infectious diseases, and he encouraged me in that area. Then he opened the door that proved to be the turning point for the rest of my career in veterinary medicine. A friend of his, Dr. Jack Hyde, the Assistant Director of the Plum Island Animal Disease Laboratory (PIADL), was looking for a veterinarian to assist with research on foot-and-mouth disease (FMD) in cattle. Dr. Fox suggested I take that job, try research on infectious diseases of cattle for a couple of years, and if I liked research, then go to graduate school for a PhD and move into an academic position at a veterinary college. If I did not like research, I could easily transition back to clinical practice. That made tremendous sense to me, and that is what I did. The Lord was in control again, opening an exceptionally large door.

Plum Island Animal Disease Laboratory

PIADL is the exotic disease research and diagnostic facility located on an island off the eastern tip of Long Island. Transportation to and from the island was provided by a three-hundred-passenger ferry boat with a twenty-minute ride each way. The purpose of PIADL was to conduct research on diseases that are not in the US to better understand these diseases and to prevent their introduction into the country.

The two years that I spent at PIADL conducting research on foot-and-mouth disease in cattle were a tremendous exposure to laboratory techniques and the field of infectious diseases in animals, especially in virology, and a solid education in isolation and disinfection techniques.

An amazing open door occurred at PIADL, which I did not fully appreciate until years later. Just as I was settling in within Lab A, the head of the lab, Dr. George Cottrell, went into surgery for severe stomach cancer and was out of work for several months. I found out later that Dr. Cottrell's usual mode of operation for a new scientist in his lab was to have that individual work on one of his research projects as a junior scientist for about three years. Then that individual could start work on his own research project. I never got set up to work on one of his research projects, and as such, I was a lone wolf in the lab. Dr. Hyde stepped in and set me up on specific research projects on FMD that PIADL wanted the answers to. He even assigned one of the experienced technicians in the lab to work with me. So, I was off and running on my own research project by the time Dr. Cottrell returned to the lab. This research project resulted in three scientific publications of which I was the senior author, and three additional publication of which I was a co-author with other scientists within Lab A.

The second open door occurred with regards to the writing and submission of scientific manuscripts for publication. After the research within the laboratory was completed for the day, you could shower out of the lab and take the bus up to the main building, which contained a library. That allowed interaction with scientists from other labs on the island. Now, here was a kid, green-as-grass when it came to writing and submission of a scientific paper. I had no training in this endeavor, and no one had told me how to proceed. In stepped Dr. John Graves, a veterinarian from Lab D. John took me under his wing and was invaluable for the training on scientific writing he gave me.

First, John walked me through the steps of identifying the appropriate journal to submit the article to, and the specifics of how that journal wanted the manuscripts written. Then, he gave me two keys to the successful writing of scientific manuscripts. The first key was to identify a person that I knew well that could be representative of the audience that would read this publication. His instruction was then to write the article specifically to that person in a way that the writing would be crystal clear to that person. His second key was to establish a "PEG" consisting of very few words that expressed the main point I wanted to convey in this article. As the article was written, I was to keep that PEG in mind and fill in around it the ancillary points and research results to support and justify the PEG.

Finally, John edited my manuscripts before submission to a journal and went over with me his suggested corrections to make the manuscript more accurate and more readable. These lessons on scientific writing were invaluable to me throughout my professional career. Thank you, Dr. Graves! And thank you, Lord, for this open door of John being my mentor.

Postdoctoral Graduate Studies

As time went on at PIADL, I found the research to be enjoyable and fulfilling, so I began making plans for possible graduate studies in virology. However, I had made a pledge to Lois and to myself that I would only go to graduate school if I could obtain a fellowship, or other financial support, that would provide reasonable support for my family. After eight years of marriage, five of which were as a professional student without any financial support, and with two children and a third on the way, I did not feel it was fair to the family for me to go off on another freebie excursion just to enhance my career.

As a veterinary student, I had gotten to know Dr. James Gillespie, a world-renowned veterinary virologist at Cornell. We had played basketball and softball together, and I had worked for him briefly on one of his research projects. In discussions with him about possible graduate studies, he said he would take me as a graduate student if I could obtain a fellowship, but he did not have a graduate fellowship available. At his suggestion, I applied for a National Institutes of Health postdoctoral fellowship, and in due time the application was approved. This NIH fellowship actually paid more than I was receiving working for the government at PIADL. So, it was back to Cornell to be trained and discipled by another "giant" in veterinary medicine—

another giant whose shoulders I would be able to stand on for a better view of the field ahead of me! Another open door! Thank you, Lord!

Bovine Winter Dysentery Thread

There is a thread that ran from my days growing up on the farm, to my time in practice in Rutland, Vermont, to my graduate studies, to my being hired as a tenure-track faculty member at Cornell College of Veterinary Medicine (CVM), and to twenty years of lectures to veterinary students. That thread was a highly contagious infectious disease of young adult, stabled dairy cows called "bovine winter dysentery," or just WD. Outbreaks of this explosive dysentery occurred during a number of winters in my family's dairy herd when I was a kid—I learned early on that it was not wise to walk behind a line of cows during a WD outbreak! I had experienced a tremendous outbreak of this disease in Vermont dairy herds during my time practicing there. The cause of this disease was unknown but thought to be a virus.

I was intrigued by WD and often wondered—could I possibly study the disease, identify the causative agent, and perhaps develop a vaccine for it? Dr. Francis Fox taught me about the veterinary aspects of this disease while I was a veterinary student, and he was fully supportive when I expressed a possible interest in studying WD during my consultation session with him before I went to PIADL.

When I started my PhD graduate studies with Dr.

Gillespie, I expressed a desire to conduct research on WD as my research project. He replied that WD was a tough disease to study and solve—he had conducted research on it off and on for fifteen years without success. He gave me one year to find an agent or to develop a diagnostic test for WD. If I was not successful, I would have to switch to another topic to finish my PhD. After one year of working on WD, I had puddled in a lot of WD manure and had transmitted the disease with fresh specimens, but I did not have an agent or a test. So, Dr. Gillespie held me to the original agreement, and I had to switch topics. Another closed door—but unbeknownst to me at the time, the Lord had another wide-open door right in front of me, and a second open door waiting for me later.

Open Door to Feline Infectious Disease Research

The year before I started my graduate studies, Dr. Gillespie had moved from the Veterinary Virus Research Institute (now the Baker Institute) off-campus to the main CVM to start a research program on feline infectious diseases. Earlier that year (1964), the feline leukemia virus (FeLV) had been isolated in Scotland and shortly after, at Cornell by Dr. Charles Rickard. This was a giant breakthrough for the study of virus-induced cancer! Dr. Gillespie rationalized that if we were to understand FeLV in the cat, then we also should understand all the other viruses that infect cats, most of which had not yet been isolated in 1964.

Dr. Gillespie developed the support laboratories and hired the technical and research staff to study feline viruses. There were two other graduate students already studying feline respiratory viruses by the time I arrived at his laboratory. Dr. Donald Kahn was conducting research on feline calicivirus (or feline picornavirus, as it was known then). Dr. Thomas Walton was conducting research on feline herpesvirus, the cause of feline viral rhinotracheitis. This feline research facility, the only one like it in the country at the time, was the precursor of the Cornell Feline Health Center, which would be founded about nine years later. So, for me, it made sense to switch from bovine viruses to feline viruses to complete my PhD, and then I could go back to studying bovine viruses and perhaps solve WD.

What I did not realize at the time was the plan the Lord had for me in the area of feline infectious diseases. I was interested in bovine viral diseases, not feline. One night, more than fifty years after starting my feline research, I was lying awake in the middle of the night thinking about how both my feline research and sharing my research information from my graduate studies with private veterinary practitioners came about. It hit me like a flash! The Holy Spirit clearly said to me. *This is the plan I had for you. I placed you in the epicenter of feline research to conduct research on feline panleukopenia, then to share these research results with veterinarians across the country, to completely control feline panleukopenia.* Wow!

The keyword for the first part of His plan was "epicenter." The Lord dropped me right in the epicenter of feline infectious diseases research in the mid-1960s! I had never thought of or ever used the word epicenter before regarding feline infectious disease research. But it is absolutely true. You see, the research program on feline infectious diseases started by Dr. Gillespie was the only one like it—not only in the United States, but in the world—at the time. Yes, individual labs and commercial vaccine companies were working on specific diseases, especially feline leukemia, but Dr. Gillespie's program was the only one that had ten to twelve graduate students and research scientists doing research on various feline infectious diseases over the first ten years of that program. It truly was the epicenter of feline infectious disease research!

The second phase of the Lord's plan was to conduct research on feline panleukopenia (FP), the most important disease of cats at the time, and the virus that causes it, feline panleukopenia virus (FPV). With the exception of one or two commercial pharmaceutical companies, no one was working on FP within Gillespie's group or within the United States in the mid-1960s. Unbeknownst to me, the Lord opened doors and set me up to conduct the key research to formulate an effective vaccination program for FP. I will expand upon that research below.

The third phase of the Lord's plan was for me to take this FP research information from our laboratory plus the information on the new and very effective FP vaccines being developed and marketed by pharmaceutical companies to veterinary practitioners throughout the country. I did not have a clue about this marvelous plan. I just started sharing our research results at whatever veterinary meeting I was invited to speak at. The Lord just opened door after door, and I naively walked through those doors wherever they led me! Again, I will expand upon this below under Teaching.

The final phase of the Lord's plan was the acquisition of complete control of FP within ten to fifteen years, not by me, but by practicing veterinarians throughout the country. FP, the most important disease in cats without question in the 1960s, would be almost totally controlled through proper vaccination by the end of the 1970s using the best vaccines or biologics in veterinary medicine—a truly remarkable achievement by the veterinary profession!

Wow! What a plan! I wish I had thought of it. But I just walked through the numerous doors that were thrown open before me, one after another from coast to coast, without knowledge about the overall plan. What a blessing to be used by God as a small part of His magnificent plan. To God be the glory, great things He has done!

Research on Feline Panleukopenia (FP)

FP is a highly contagious viral disease of cats characterized by sudden onset, fever, vomiting, diarrhea, severe depression, severe dehydration, and high mortality. I used the "four Ds" to summarize FP to my veterinary students—Diarrhea, Dehydration, Depression, and Death. The name "panleukopenia" is derived from the severe depression of all white blood cells during the clinical phase of the disease. "Pan" refers to everything, all, or total; "leuko" refers to the leukocytes or white blood cells; "penia" refers to lowering, suppression, or below normal.

In 1964, the year before I started my graduate studies, Robert Johnson in the United Kingdom successfully isolated the virus from a snow leopard with FP. He identified the key factor for the isolation of the virus in cell culture—the absolute need for a rapidly dividing cell for the virus to replicate. This is an incredibly unique factor for virus replication.

No one in Gillespie's group, nor anyone in the entire country at that time, as far as I knew, was working on FP. So I decided (or rather, the Lord decided for me as part of His magnificent plan), with Dr. Gillespie's approval, to study FP by looking at the transmission of passive or temporary immunity from the mother to her kittens via the colostrum or early milk, and how this passive immunity affected vaccination. Dr. Gillespie had worked this out for canine distemper in the dog, and now I hopefully could reproduce his work in the cat for FP, the most important and deadly disease of cats at the time.

The hypothesis involved several factors. First, the anti-FPV antibodies or passive immunity transferred from the immune queen to her kittens through the colostrum or early milk provide solid but temporary protection against FPV; second, this passive immunity will also block FP vaccines until it wanes or is eliminated; and lastly, once the passive immunity is gone, the kitten becomes susceptible to infection and disease. Thus, the aim of this research was to establish the best age to vaccinate kittens against FP.

To test this hypothesis, the plan was to obtain pregnant cats, determine the immune level or serum antibody titer of the queens, and determine the antibody titers of the kittens weekly from birth until four months of age. Periodically, the protective ability of these passive antibodies in each kitten would be determined by exposure to FPV.

The bottom line, or the desired research results of this study, would be to establish the best age to vaccinate kittens against FP and the best vaccination protocol to prevent this devastating disease in the most cats possible.

Several problems had to be overcome to conduct the proposed research. Remember, this was 1966, and research on diseases of cats was in its infancy—the feline leukemia research program at Cornell was just getting underway. There were no disease-free research cats available, no standard cages were available to house research cats and kittens, and there was not an isolation facility to house cats that were infectious. There was no oversight committee to approve research on laboratory animals. As I look back, I am amazed at how the unique doors were opened in each of these areas. Thank you, Lord!

First, I needed a source of pregnant cats. I worked part-time for a local veterinarian on Saturdays, helping him out with dairy farm calls. Most dairy farms had several cats in the barns to keep the mouse and rat populations under control. As I was doing pregnancy checks on cows, or doing tuberculosis testing or calfhood vaccinations for brucellosis, I would spot an obviously pregnant cat. The farmer would usually gladly sell me the pregnant cat for five dollars.

To house the cats, I obtained the use of some old rabbit cages which I could set up in the physiology barn. Later, when it came time to challenge the immunity of the kittens, I was graciously allowed to use one of the two "isolation" rooms in the large animal clinic.

Although this was not an ideal situation, it did enable studies to be completed. In later years, after the federally mandated Institutional Animal Care and Use Committee (IACUC) was established, this research plan would not have been approved. However, since there were no restrictions or mandated guidelines at the time, we did the best we could under the circumstances and proceeded with the research, taking the best care we could of the health and welfare of the cats and kittens in the study. Again, open doors!

The very first pregnant farm cat that I purchased and her litter of three kittens essentially answered all parts of the hypothesis! It is rare to have the first attempt at a research project work out so beautifully. But, of course, with the Lord, all things are possible. From there it was just an expansion of numbers and working out specific details.

The FP studies turned out to be an excellent research project, and the information was very useful for the development of new and improved vaccines, the development of vaccination protocols for the cat, and helping practicing veterinarians who were just beginning to take the cat seriously as a patient in their practices. It was a privilege to share these research findings with practicing veterinarians from coast to coast and even some foreign veterinarians in Europe and Asia. How this came about will be expanded upon later under Teaching.

The FP vaccines that were developed by commercial companies in the late 1960s and early 1970s, and the proper use of these vaccines in the cat, totally eliminated FP in most cat populations. FP now only occurs rarely, such as in adoption shelters or in feral, unvaccinated cats. Most young veterinarians today have never seen a clinical case of FP. To have played a small part in eliminating this scourge of cats is one of the most satisfying aspects of my career in veterinary medicine. Thanks be to God for His marvelous plan!

CHAPTER 6

Faculty Member, Cornell University College of Veterinary Medicine

Faculty Position

Back to that thread of WD in my career: during the spring of my third year of graduate studies (1968), the Lord suddenly and amazingly opened a huge door for me, one that I did not even know existed at the time. People are always amazed when I tell them about my thirty-second interview for a tenure track faculty position at the Cornell CVM. One morning I was working at my desk in my cubby hole office in the back of my lab when Dr. Gillespie appeared in the doorway. He said that New York State had approved a new tenure track faculty position in the recently passed college budget for the study of winter dysentery in cattle. Then he asked if I would be interested in this position. "Absolutely," I replied. Dr. Gillespie then said, "Okay, you've got it. Congratulations! Stop in at the department chairman's office and sign some papers." That is how I joined the faculty at the CVM, where I spent thirty amazing years as a faculty member! There was no application or search for a job on my part, no international search, no interview, no seminar, no affirmative action, and no job description. Just finish my PhD degree, and then conduct research on WD. Talk about a wide-open door! Only the Lord could have orchestrated this amazing scenario. Thank you, Lord!

I went home that evening and said to Lois and our three boys, "Well, we are staying in Ithaca." I then shared with them the amazing day. I had not started to search for a job since I had thought it would take another year to finish my graduate studies. We had briefly talked about how nice it would be if we could stay in Ithaca after graduate school, but we did not have a clue about any possibility of that happening. We had lived in Ithaca for seven years at that point, four years during which I had been in veterinary school and three years in graduate school, so we knew and liked the area. Our two older sons, Duane, and John, were enrolled in Ithaca schools, so they would not have to move and change schools.

Before I could join the faculty, a small task was ahead of me—finishing and defending my thesis within three years instead of four. Over the next few months, the research was concluded—or, at least, it was conducted to the point of a convenient pause area. Dr. Gillespie and my committee were fully aware that this was an unusual and unique situation—I already had a faculty position and a designated date at which I would move into that position. They wanted a condensed form of the thesis that would include giving the facts and research results to date. There were good research results with valuable information, but there were still some areas that normally would have been expanded and completed before the thesis defense. The committee agreed that I could continue the research after I joined the faculty to fill in the areas where more data were needed, and then the results could be submitted for publication. Wow! This was part of that marvelous open door to a wonderful faculty position.

The thesis was handwritten, and the department kindly assigned one of the department secretaries to type my thesis—this was years before computers came onto the scene. Graphs were handmade using an archaic system of running sticky dotted or dashed lines on a plastic sheet over graph paper. Photos were taken of these graphs, and the photos were mounted on pages within the thesis. In August 1968, the thesis was finished and defended, and the PhD degree awarded. I joined the faculty of the CVM as Assistant Professor of Virology on September 1, 1968.

As I look back at my time as a faculty member at the CVM at Cornell, I am amazed at the wonderful opportunities that opened to me—more of those amazing open doors. As I relate the accomplishments and experiences as a faculty member, I do so not to show "how great thou art" or to say, "look what I have accomplished." Rather, I do so to show how the Lord was able to take this naive farm boy and transition him into a cog in this wonderful profession of veterinary medicine, hopefully, to provide some benefits to the profession and the health and welfare of a portion of His animal kingdom. I have no false illusions about my own grandeur, but I do have a tremendous awareness of the grace and greatness of our Lord, and how He can use a simple and imperfect person to accomplish His amazing purposes—how He can open doors that would seem to be impossible to open!

Lois and I became avid followers of Southern Gospel music, especially the music of the Gaither Vocal Band, starting a few years before I retired. Many of these gospel songs cut through the hustle and bustle of our daily lives to drive home a message about daily Christian living. Throughout this book, I have listed some of our favorite songs that are now available on YouTube. I hope the reader will enjoy watching and listening to them. The words of a Southern Gospel song sum up the unmerited grace God has bestowed upon me throughout my career: *"Greatly blessed. Highly favored. Imperfect, but forgiven, child of God."*— Gaither Vocal Band. *Greatly Blessed, Highly Favored.* https://www.youtube.com/watch?v=R4yARnWHeVs. Lyrics by Larry Gatlin and Bill Gaither.

Also, the marvelous hymn written by Fanny Crosby (1820-1915) says it all: "To God be the glory, great things He hath done."

I did not have a specific job description during my years as a faculty member, so early on I just plotted my road as I thought best, grasping opportunities or addressing needs as they occurred—or so I thought, not realizing that the Lord was actually guiding me. It was only toward the end of my career that everyone had to give a detailed annual report to the department chair, outlining what had been accomplished during the past year and what the plans were for the coming year.

Research

Good research from a laboratory reflects the excellent staff making up that laboratory. The Lord greatly blessed my laboratory with outstanding staff, and I would like to acknowledge three of those individuals.

Jim Buck was an animal caretaker hired by Dr. Gillespie during the time of my graduate studies and continued providing animal care for me for several years after I joined the faculty. He was a dedicated worker and a great individual and always provided excellent animal care. He always provided excellent assistance to any of the scientists working with the cats.

Eleanor Tompkins was a lab tech for me for fifteen years. Eleanor was the most reliable, pleasant, and consistent staff worker I have encountered. Although she had no laboratory experience, she was hired by Dr. Gillespie in the early days of the feline research program. She and her husband owned a farm, she had raised her family on that farm, and she felt it was time to work outside the farm. Dr. Gillespie intended her to work with one of the other graduate students, but he resisted training an inexperienced lab tech. The wife of one of our DVM students was working as a lab tech in my lab, and she was excellent. Dr. Gillespie asked if I would take on Eleanor in my lab and train her so the DVM student's wife could work for the other grad student. I agreed—one of the best decisions I have made.

She quietly but quickly picked up every lab technique I asked her to perform. Our FP assays were labor-intense and required reading slides to identify the presence of the virus. At first, I had to read all these slides, but Eleanor soon took over the reading of all the slides, which saved me hours each day.

The third individual is Cordell Geissinger, who worked in my lab as a research tech for twenty-five years, retiring at the same time I retired. Cordell, an experienced research tech who had worked in other labs at Cornell for several years, joined our lab on an NIH antiviral contract. He handled all the animal-related duties of all our studies, and when Eleanor Tompkins retired, Cordell also assumed the lab tech duties she had been doing. There is no question that the Lord directed and oversaw the hiring of Cordell. He is a devout Christian who grew up in a Mennonite family. Whatever, and whenever, the research protocol required, either working with the cats on study or doing testing within the lab, Cordell always took care of what needed to be done. We became good friends and neighbors, and we served together on the elder board at our church. To God be the glory.

Bovine Winter Dysentery

For the first ten years on the faculty, I continued research on feline viral diseases, plus limited research on bovine WD during the winter months when herd outbreaks occurred in the Ithaca area. Money to support the WD research was difficult to obtain. The first year, the budget from the state paid for my salary, plus four hundred dollars to support WD research. That was the last funding the state provided for WD research—other than providing for my salary. Limited funds were obtained from various sources, but nothing sufficient to fund a meaningful research program.

Grants that would support a meaningful research program on WD were submitted to the National Institutes of Health, but they were never approved. I tried to make the case that this explosive intestinal infectious disease outbreak in cows was a good model for explosive gastrointestinal outbreaks in humans. NIH would not buy this argument. Years later, look at what has happened on cruise ships with the explosive gastrointestinal outbreaks of norovirus. Interestingly, norovirus outbreaks in humans are more common in winter, and a lay term for norovirus is "winter vomiting bug."

As the tremendous interest in feline infectious diseases continued to increase each year—as did the frustrations of trying to obtain funding for the bovine research—I finally threw in the towel and concentrated solely on the feline research. While one door was wide open, the other was slammed shut. The feline infectious disease research was definitely in the Lord's plan, but, apparently, WD research was not.

Dr. Francis Fox never forgave me for abandoning the WD research and "going to the cats," as he always informed each class during his annual WD lecture. I have always believed, but never had it confirmed, that Dr. Fox played a key role in getting my faculty position into the college budget. The last WD research we conducted was done by my former graduate student, Dr. Tak Hoshino, who identified an apparently new coronavirus by electron microscopy of WD fecal samples. We thought we had the answer to WD, but a check of "normal" fecal samples showed the same coronavirus. Unfortunately for us, Dr. Hoshino left at that point for a position at the National Institutes of Health, so we had no one to run the electron microscope, nor did we have the research funds to hire a new person, and therefore we could not sort out the findings any further. A few years later, workers in Ohio identified the cause of WD to be a coronavirus. We were so close to solving the disease, but unfortunately, that is the way research works out sometimes. So that was the end of the WD thread for me—a closed door. This is the most disappointing part of my viral research studies.

Feline Panleukopenia

After joining the faculty, the research on FP continued to fill in those areas that had not been fully completed prior to the thesis defense. Once this research was completed, manuscripts were written and submitted to scientific journals for publication.

The main emphasis for the next several years was on the new FP vaccines being developed by several commercial veterinary pharmaceutical companies. For most of these vaccines, we just evaluated the level of immunity produced by the vaccines after they arrived on the market. In some cases, we worked with the company before they marketed the vaccine and if there was a specific problem afterward.

In 1975, I had one of those "What now?" moments. There were several excellent FP vaccines on the market, veterinarians were routinely vaccinating all cats, and FP was basically totally controlled by the vaccines. I remember thinking, *we know all we need to know about FP and the parvovirus that causes it, FPV, so it is time to move on to something else.* Yeah, right. So, we made the decision to make an all-out attack on feline infectious peritonitis, which was then, and still is today, an unbelievably bad and usually fatal disease of cats.

In 1977, two years after my illustrious conclusion about FP and FPV, a slight mutation occurred in the genome of the FP virus such that it now was highly contagious to dogs. This new virus, canine parvovirus, went worldwide within just a few months. The canine population was totally susceptible, and this new disease was disastrous to the canine population, especially young pups.

There was a mad scramble to develop, evaluate, and patent vaccines to protect dogs against this new virus. The feline vaccines for FPV, and the closely related mink enteritis virus (MEV) vaccines for mink, were quickly shown to produce good but not perfect protection in dogs. There was suddenly a tremendous shortage of FP and MEV vaccines, as veterinarians were using these vaccines off-label to protect dogs.

The Baker Institute at the Cornell CVM has been

the leading laboratory in the world for the study of infectious diseases of the dog ever since its founding in 1950. Several world-famous veterinary virologists at the Baker Institute led the charge against canine parvovirus. They developed and patented excellent vaccines, which were then licensed to be marketed by veterinary pharmaceutical companies.

Our laboratory briefly collaborated with the canine virologists at the Baker Institute during the initial isolation of the canine virus and the initial studies using the feline vaccines. After that, we stepped back and returned to feline studies, leaving canine studies to those at the Baker Institute. In retrospect, I believe it was the leading of the Lord that stopped me from pursuing the canine studies—He shut that door completely and kept me within the feline studies as part of His plan for my career. One more great example of how the Lord opens and closes doors in our lives.

Adoption shelter feline vaccines

As I look back over my career, I am constantly amazed as I now recognize more and more of the open doors the Lord provided. Often, it was an incidental situation that was unplanned but which, in retrospect, provided invaluable information for veterinary medicine. Here is one of those amazing open doors.

Viral diseases of cats in adoption shelters in the 1960s and early 1970s were rampant, especially FP and upper respiratory diseases. The only vaccine that was sometimes used was the crude tissue origin FP or feline distemper vaccine. The newer and more effective cell culture origin FP vaccines were just beginning to be available, and the upper respiratory combined vaccines for feline herpesvirus and feline calicivirus had not yet been developed.

In 1970, I was approached by the director of the local adoption shelter in Ithaca. This shelter did not have a vaccination program for cats, and FP was a severe and constant problem. Many, many cats, especially kittens, developed FP. Many died of FP or were euthanized because they were sick and could not be adopted. His question was a simple one: *What is the best vaccination program we can set up to prevent FP in the shelter?*

Since, to the best of my knowledge, no one had evaluated the new FP vaccines in a shelter situation, my answer was simple: I do not know. But I followed up this answer with a proposal: *If you are willing to work with our lab, we can set up a simple clinical study to answer that question.* He was more than willing, so a study was set up. There was no funding to support this study, so it had to be set up within the working conditions of the local shelter, and it was before the Cornell Feline Health Center was established.

Dr. Leo Wuori had recently moved to Ithaca and set up the only private small animal veterinary clinic in Ithaca, and he became the veterinarian for the shelter. Dr. Wuori agreed to do the vaccinations—but at his clinic, not at the shelter. Not an ideal situation, since the new cats arriving at the shelter were taken to Dr.

Wuori's clinic once a day for vaccination. The best situation would have been to vaccinate the cats immediately as they entered the shelter.

There were three types of FP vaccines available on the market at this time. The first was the old, crude, feline tissue-origin, inactivated, feline distemper vaccines that were developed in the mid-1930s; the second was the new cell-culture-origin, inactivated FP vaccines; and the third was the new cell-culture-origin, modified live-virus FP vaccines. There was also available at this time the old feline distemper hyperimmune serum, which was produced as a byproduct in the production of the old tissue-origin vaccines. This hyperimmune serum was used in some shelters to provide temporary immunity to FP or to try to treat clinical cases of FP (usually unsuccessfully).

Our lab obtained a supply of each of the three types of vaccines and the hyperimmune serum and established five "vaccines" labeled only as Vaccine A, Vaccine B, Vaccine C, Vaccine D, and Vaccine E. One of these "vaccines" was a placebo vaccine to serve as an unvaccinated control. My technician and I were the only ones that knew which vaccine was which.

The vaccines were supplied to Dr. Wuori along with a self-addressed card to my lab which included information about the identity of the cat, the vaccine that was used, and the date of vaccination. As the shelter cats were presented to Dr. Wuori for vaccination, he would evaluate each cat, and every fifth cat deemed to be healthy was vaccinated with Vaccine A; the next cat was vaccinated with Vaccine B; etc.

When the cat was adopted from the shelter, the new owner was given the vaccine card and specific instructions to take the cat to their local veterinarian one month later to give that cat's card to the veterinarian and to have the cat re-vaccinated for FP. If the cat became ill before one month, of course, the owner was to take the cat to a veterinarian. The veterinarian made a clinical evaluation of whether that cat had remained healthy or had developed clinical FP. The veterinarian signed the card, which was then returned to my lab.

This study continued until we had received approximately fifty cards for cats vaccinated with each vaccine. We tabulated the results, and these results became a vital part of every lecture that was given on FP from that time on.

The results:

Vaccine Type	% of Cats that Developed Clinical FP
•Placebo vaccine	44%
•Inactivated tissue-origin vaccine	28%
•Inactivated cell-culture-origin vaccine	14%
•Modified live-virus vaccine	7%
•Feline distemper hyperimmune serum*	4%

*In addition to the 4% of cats in this group that developed clinical FP, a few cats came down with the disease four weeks or more after vaccination. When the study was set up, I queried the director as to how long the cats were held in the shelter if they were not adopted before they were euthanized. I knew cats in this group would only receive temporary immunity and would have to receive another vaccination in two weeks for their protection. The director assured me that the shelter never kept cats for more than two weeks. When I raised the question about these particular cats later, his response was, "Oh, these were really nice cats, so we decided to hold them longer."

So, the answer to the question "What is the best FP vaccine for a shelter situation?" was crystal clear. The modified live-virus vaccines produced the best and fastest protection. If the vaccines had been given ASAP after the cats entered the shelter, the results would have been even better.

This brief study also confirmed what we already knew. FP was a major problem in shelters. In this case, without an effective vaccine, 44% of the shelter cats developed clinical disease, usually with severe and often fatal results. Truly, this was the most severe and devastating disease in cats at that time.

This shelter was typical of local shelters in the 1960s and early 1970s. Since that time, this shelter has become a state-of-the-art no-kill shelter with excellent facilities and programs to maintain the healthiest possible cats and dogs. Shelter medicine programs have been established at most of the veterinary colleges in the US, including at the Cornell CVM. One of the shining lights in veterinary medicine is the tremendous advances that have been made in shelter medicine over the past fifty years! I give thanks to the Lord for opening another door, which allowed me to play a small part in providing research data to assist in the great improvement of shelter medicine. A nice open door!

Feline Respiratory Vaccines

Research on the feline respiratory viruses, feline herpesvirus (FHV) and feline calicivirus (FCV), was a major part of Dr. Gillespie's feline infectious disease program. This research provided much of the original scientific information about these two important feline viruses. While there is only one serotype or strain of FHV, there are many strains and subtypes of FCV. Dr. Gillespie facilitated a large, multi-institutional study on the various strains of FCV in order to select the best strains for vaccine production.

While research on feline respiratory viruses was not a major part of studies in our laboratory, we did work with Pitman-Moore during and after their development and marketing the first feline respiratory vaccine for FHV and FCV. I was a consultant to Pitman-Moore for several years, so it was logical to be involved in evaluating this new and exciting vaccine.

As information about this and other new respiratory vaccines became available, this information was added to the CE programs presented to veterinarians.

One study that was done on this respiratory vaccine was a duration of immunity (DOI) study to determine how long this vaccine would protect cats against these two viruses. This study was supposed to go for one year but was prematurely ended because of an unfortunate circumstance that I will expand upon next.

Disinfectants vs. Feline Viruses

This is another example of how the Lord took an unfortunate turn of events and with it, opened a new door. The incidental study resulted in information that became valuable beyond anything anticipated at the time.

The immunity study on the new feline respiratory vaccine for FHV and FCV, mentioned above, was a year-long study involving a significant number of cats. The cats were housed in state-of-the-art isolation cages within the new laboratory animal facilities at the CVM. Each sealed cage had its own air supply, and, theoretically, infectious disease studies on different viruses could be conducted in neighboring cages without any transfer of agents between cages—that is, if the procedures set up for the specific studies are followed to the letter and if the disinfectant used to clean the cages is highly effective for those particular agents.

In this study, conducted in the mid-1970s, the cats were vaccinated according to protocol, and then blood samples were periodically taken to measure the antibody titers, or levels of immunity. About halfway through this study, preliminary results did not make any sense. Something had gone wrong. Control cats, which should not have been infected, had somehow become infected with FCV, and had developed immunity. This negated the whole study, and the study had to be terminated.

But what went wrong? There was always the possibility of human error, but we could not determine any obvious flaw in the way the cats were handled daily. Then we tested the disinfectant/cleaning solution that was used throughout the entire laboratory animal facility. To our shock, this disinfectant had absolutely no activity against FCV! So, the routine daily feed, water, and cleaning process simply transmitted FCV from one cage to the next.

A check of the literature revealed a complete lack of any information on disinfectants for caliciviruses. What to do? We were on our own and would have to find the answer ourselves. It would not help the DOI study that had just been terminated, but the information was vital for any future FCV studies.

In retrospect, this is when the Lord stepped in and guided us! If we were going to test potential disinfectants against feline calicivirus, we should also look at feline parvovirus (feline panleukopenia virus) and feline herpesvirus. We knew FPV was very resistant and probably would be resistant to several disinfectants, and FHV was quite labile and probably would be inactivated by most disinfectants.

I asked my research tech, Cordell, to round up all the disinfectants, surgical scrubs, soaps, antiseptics, cage-cleaning products, and anything else he could find in the laboratory animal facility, the clinics, and various labs. I laughed when he returned and showed me all the products he had found—a two-shelved lab cart completely filled with a weird collection of bottles, jars, and various other containers. Cordell had some work lined up!

Cordell tested all the products against the three feline viruses, at varying dilutions, including the recommended dilution. When the results were in, we arranged the results into the categories the products fell into. The results were eye-opening and clear. As expected, herpesvirus was susceptible to most all the agents, and calicivirus was fairly resistant but susceptible to a few agents. We had the answer for the agent(s) to be used in future FCV studies.

Feline parvovirus was completely resistant to almost all the disinfectants in this study! The 70% isopropyl alcohol, which was routinely used in most veterinary clinics to clean exam tables between patients, had absolutely no action on the virus. The best disinfectant by far was ordinary, regular Clorox®, 5.5% sodium hypochlorite, at a dilution of 1:32. A 1:64 dilution was only partially effective, and a 1:128 dilution had absolutely no effect on the virus.

Now, the amazing and unexpected. This study was conducted about two years before the slight mutation of feline parvovirus so that it now could infect canine cells. The new virus disease of dogs, canine parvovirus, went worldwide in a matter of months, and it was devastating for a completely susceptible dog population. Veterinary clinics were suddenly hit with this new disease, and many dogs died. It was a genuine canine pandemic!

Disinfectants that were commonly used at that time in veterinary clinics to disinfect cages, floors, food and water dishes, and runs were totally ineffective against this new virus. Since the feline and canine parvoviruses are essentially the same, the information that the Lord had guided us to obtain for the feline virus could be immediately used to disinfect clinics, kennels, and adoption shelters when an outbreak of the new virus occurred. So, the results of this disinfectant study to obtain information for future research studies were immediately provided to the veterinary profession far and wide.

A few months after the initial outbreak occurred in the Cornell CVM clinic, which had been stopped using the Clorox disinfectant, another outbreak occurred. I received a call for help from the clinic, and a quick check on what happened solved the problem. The Clorox disinfectant being used was a bit irritating to the animal caretakers, so they diluted out the Clorox to the point where it had no effect on the virus. By switching back to the recommended concentration of Clorox, the outbreak was halted.

New canine parvovirus vaccines became available ASAP, and the disease is now fairly well-controlled through the routine vaccination of all dogs.

Feline Infectious Peritonitis

Feline infectious peritonitis (FIP) is a severe, usually fatal disease of cats caused by a feline coronavirus (FCoV). Peritonitis refers to the severe, inflammatory tissue reaction that occurs in the abdomen.

FIP was first reported in the early 1960s in Boston, Massachusetts, and the first case seen at the Cornell CVM was in the late 1960s. FIP is often difficult to diagnose until late in the disease process. Until just recently, there was no effective treatment. A new antiviral treatment may now be on the horizon. There is only one FIP vaccine that has been licensed, and this vaccine has little if any beneficial effect. So, the disease is still one of the most feared diseases, especially in breeding catteries.

In 1975, we at the CFHC decided to launch a major research effort on FIP. The goals of this research were to (1) increase our understanding of this terrible disease, (2) try to develop an accurate diagnostic test, and (3) attempt to develop an effective vaccine.

A check of the graduate students listed later in this book will show a significant number of thesis research projects on FIP. This group of research scientists did a phenomenal job over a period of twenty years pushing back the cloud of mystery over this disease and helping to develop tests that could detect the FCoV. Through the research at the CFHC, and several other labs at other universities, a great deal has been learned about this disease. But we are not home yet.

FIP is an immune-mediated disease—that is, the

immune system in an infected cat tends to work against the cat instead of working to protect the cat. Several of the graduate students in my lab over this twenty-year period were instrumental in working out many of the details in how this immune-mediated enhancement, or antibody-dependent enhancement, occurs in FIP.

I believe the Lord directed me and my technicians to tackle the studies to develop a vaccine for FIP. A great deal of research was conducted, often supported by grants from various commercial companies, and we did develop a possible vaccine. This possible vaccine turned out to be similar to the one vaccine that is licensed. However, we did not feel our vaccine was safe enough nor effective enough to release, so it was never turned over to a commercial company. It has been almost thirty years since that lone FIP vaccine was licensed, and no other FIP vaccine has been developed.

The Lord provided several open doors to small gains in FIP research over those twenty years, but for whatever reason, the large open door that would lead to an effective vaccine did not occur, or if it did, I completely missed it. FIP is a difficult disease, and like cancer, advances come a little at a time.

After they escaped from Egypt, the Israelites wandered through the desert for forty years, totally reliant upon the Lord for direction, food, and protection until He opened the door to the promised land. We only wandered in the desert of FIP for twenty years—did we need another twenty years?

Teaching

Teaching was not on my radar. It was not on my bucket list of possible career options. I never took an education class, and I took only one minor public speaking class at UMass. Amazing how things can change, especially when the Lord is directing things and opening doors as part of His plan.

During my graduate studies at the CVM, all graduate students were required to assist in the bacteriology and virology labs. No lecturing was involved; the work consisted only of assisting the veterinary students one-on-one in their understanding of what each lab was about.

At the miraculous open door where I was "handed" a tenure track faculty position within the Department of Microbiology, as described above, there was no mention of teaching. It was verbally communicated to be only a research position. There was not even a written job description alluding to the percentage of time specified to research, teaching, or clinics/service.

Continuing Education for Practicing Veterinarians

Prior to the isolation and identification of the feline leukemia virus (FeLV) in the mid-1960s, almost no research had been done on the infectious diseases of the cat. Suddenly, there was great interest in FeLV research, and, consequently, interest in other feline infectious diseases. I arrived at Dr. Gillespie's laboratory just as this interest was starting to explode, and I consider it a great privilege to have been a small part of this bourgeoning interest. It was like falling into a great vacuum—veterinary practitioners were keen to grasp any information that would help them control the deluge of infectious diseases in their cat patients. I was tremendously blessed to be one of the messengers to the practicing veterinarians throughout the United States, and even abroad, of the new information on diagnosing and controlling feline infectious diseases. I just chalked it up as good fortune to be at the right place at the right time. I had no clue until many years later that this was part of that magnificent career plan the Lord had made for me.

In the 1960s and 1970s, there were many veterinary pharmaceutical companies in the US, some large, but most very small. These companies, mostly in the Midwest, started as companies to provide hog cholera vaccines and antiserums. Hog cholera was a tremendous problem in swine industries at the time. As this disease began to be controlled and eventually eliminated, these companies started looking to develop other vaccines. The new interest in feline infectious diseases was a logical next step.

What developed was a string of invitations—open doors—to visit these pharmaceutical companies and discuss the details of the various feline diseases and the viruses that caused them. We did not develop any feline vaccines at Cornell during these early days, but we were able to provide a few virus isolates that could be used for vaccines, and we were also able to evaluate several of these new vaccines developed by various companies. This information about the efficacy of these new vaccines was passed on to practicing veterinarians during the many lectures and continuing education programs on feline infectious diseases throughout the country.

One thing that we were able to do was provide companies with the only feline cell line that was available at that time to assist companies in developing the various vaccines. Dr. Robert Crandall, a close friend of Dr. Gillespie, had done research on feline respiratory diseases and isolated the first feline herpesvirus. As part of his research, he had developed from primary feline kidney cells what he called the CRFK cell line. As a military officer and veterinarian, when he was relocated to South America for a tour of duty, he sent his cell line to Dr. Gillespie for safekeeping. This feline cell line was made available to companies for feline vaccine development. I have no idea how many companies received this cell line, but it was sent all over the country, and there were several international shipments. It played a key role in the development of new feline vaccines.

As my graduate research began to produce some interesting and valuable information on vaccination of cats against FP (as described previously), I was asked to give seminars on these research results. First, I had to give a seminar to the CVM graduate faculty and my graduate committee as part of my thesis defense. Second, I had to give a seminar at a meeting of the local county veterinary medical society at the CVM.

My first venture out of town was to Boston, Massachusetts, to give a seminar to the staff of Angell Memorial Animal Hospital at an invitation from Dr. Jean Holzworth (Cornell CVM 1950). Dr. Holzworth, who I have affectionately called "The Mother of Feline Medicine," was without question the most prominent feline veterinarian of her time. She helped me considerably with my graduate research on FP, and the control of FP was very dear to her heart. It was after the death of her favorite cat to FP in 1943 that she made the career-changing decision to give up teaching classics at Mount Holyoke College in Massachusetts (despite having both MS and PhD degrees in Latin) and pursue a new career in veterinary medicine specifically to treat cats. This was unheard of in the 1940s!

I found these seminars to be enjoyable and rewarding. After all, I was presenting information from my research and making recommendations to veterinarians on how they could better control, through proper vaccination, the most important scourge of cats at that time. A few short years before, I had been in their situation, and I recalled vividly how frustrating it was dealing with FP in practice. As new cell-culture-origin vaccines, both inactivated and modified-live-virus, became available, we tested them for efficacy. This data gave me a solid cache of information to pass on to the veterinarians.

It was amazing to see how the incidence of FP dramatically decreased following the widespread vaccination programs using these new, excellent vaccines. Within ten to fifteen years, the most important disease of cats, which was ubiquitous within cat populations with a death rate of at least 50%, became almost totally controlled and prevented via proper vaccination! Little did I know (until fifty years later), this was all part of God's plan to control FP.

As new research information became available about other infectious diseases of cats, both from Cornell researchers and from researchers at other universities, it was logical to expand the seminars and discuss these other infectious agents and their diseases. So, the one-hour seminars on FP morphed into several-hour and even whole-day continuing education (CE) courses for practicing veterinarians on "Feline Infectious Diseases."

Other speakers were picking up the mantel, and most large meetings now had a section on feline infectious diseases, and then on other aspects of feline diseases and feline practice. The interest in feline diseases and feline medicine was increasing by leaps and bounds. The decade of the 1970s was when feline medicine came of age.

The first respiratory vaccine for feline herpesvirus, also known as feline viral rhinotracheitis (FVR), and feline calicivirus was licensed in 1975 by the veterinary pharmaceutical company Pitman-Moore. This vaccine was combined with the MLV FP vaccine to give the triple MLV vaccine known as FVRCP, which became a core vaccine to be used annually in all cats. Our lab worked closely with Pitman-Moore, testing the safety and efficacy of this vaccine as it moved toward marketing. This safety and efficacy research information could then be passed on to practicing veterinarians during the numerous seminars and CE programs throughout the country. Other triple vaccines for these agents eventually became available, but veterinarians continued to use the code FVRCP whenever a cat was vaccinated with a triple vaccine for these three viruses, regardless of what vaccine was used.

Diagnostic tests for feline leukemia virus infection became available in the 1970s, thus providing a reliable method of diagnosing and controlling FeLV. A test and removal program was developed by Dr. Bill Hardy, the developer of the original gold standard FeLV diagnostic test. At the beginning of the 1970s, purebred catteries had an incidence of 20%-33% infection with FeLV. These cats had FeLV persistently in their blood, and they were constantly shedding a highly infectious virus. Many of these FeLV-infected cats died of leukemia or other cancers (like lymphosarcoma) caused by the virus, or from FeLV-related diseases. With Dr. Hardy's test and removal program, catteries across the country were able to completely eliminate FeLV from their facilities. All this scientific information provided more educational material to be passed on to veterinarians in the various seminars.

Information was beginning to appear about the new disease feline infectious peritonitis (FIP), a disease that was difficult to diagnose, had no effective treatment or vaccine, and was uniformly fatal. Our laboratory made a major effort to study this disease, starting in 1975 and continuing for the next twenty years. With the outstanding efforts of several excellent graduate students and research staff, we learned a great deal about the disease. Instead of cats developing an effective immune response against the virus, they were developing an autoimmune response that made the disease worse and eventually fatal. Unfortunately, we were unable to develop a good diagnostic test, an effective treatment, or a safe and effective vaccine. Several excellent laboratories within the US, Europe, and Japan actively studied FIP during this period, and several are still studying FIP at the time of this writing. Fortunately, recently an apparently effective antiviral treatment has been developed.

With the rapidly expanding interest in feline medicine, especially regarding feline infectious diseases, practicing veterinarians were constantly eager to obtain the latest information about these diseases. I continued to receive invitations to give seminars or CE programs at local, state, regional, and national veterinary meetings. On average, there was an invitation to speak at least once every month at one of these organizations. I did not have an organized plan, nor did I ever advertise to speak. It was just a steady stream of invitations—a steady stream of open doors! I just took it one day at a time and did not have a clue that the Lord was opening so many of these doors or that it was part of His plan for me.

So, this was how my teaching career was born—not in a classroom before veterinary students, but on local, state, and national meeting stages before graduate veterinarians who were anxious to learn the latest in controlling infectious diseases in the cats they were seeing daily in their practices. It wasn't based on some master plan that I had concocted with all the details laid out in advance, but rather guided by the "unmerited favor to be at the right place at the right time"—or so I thought until the Lord blessed me fifty years later with the clear knowledge that in fact it had been the plan the Lord had for me all along. Praise be to God for His master plan for my career, and for those marvelous "open doors" that were constantly placed before me!

There were three seminars in those early days of the late 1960s that still are vivid in my mind for the learning aspect that each seminar presented to me. First, my first seminar at a state meeting was at the annual meeting of the New York State Veterinary Medical Society at a conference center in the Catskills. Dr. Bill Hardy and I were to present the feline medicine portion of the meeting. Bill had new information that the recently isolated and named feline leukemia virus (FeLV) was in fact contagious and transmissible between cats. Although the information had not been published yet, news had gotten around to practicing veterinarians. I was to follow up his seminar with my FP seminar. As Bill and I were talking before the meeting, we mused that the attendance probably would not be very great. After all, this was a feline program, and feline programs were not of interest to practicing veterinarians in the late 1960s—or so we assumed. The meeting room for the feline program was a small side room with three rows of chairs providing seating for about thirty people. When the meeting time arrived, to our amazement, or at least to my amazement, the room was packed far beyond capacity, with many veterinarians standing. What an eye-opener that was for me to see just how ravenous the practicing veterinarians were to grasp any information about feline infectious diseases. *Perhaps, I thought then, I should drop my original plan to get back to working on viral diseases of cattle, and instead concentrate on feline infectious diseases?*

The second learning seminar was to discuss the efficacy of a new FP vaccine that was being sold by one of the large, well-known pharmaceutical companies. I was contacted by a veterinarian heading the animal division of this company, who stated they had a problem with their new vaccine, and that cats vaccinated with this vaccine were later dying from FP. The veterinarian asked if I would help them by evaluating the efficacy of this new vaccine.

In the first few years after the FP virus was isolated in cell cultures in the laboratory, companies were anxiously attempting to make better and more efficacious FP vaccines to replace the old tissue-origin vaccine that had been available for many years. Since in our laboratory we were routinely running assays to determine the immunity, or anti-FPV antibody titers, in the sera of cats, this challenge would be straightforward for us. The company provided doses of vaccine, and we vaccinated several FPV antibody-negative kittens. After an appropriate post-vaccination time, we obtained blood samples from these kittens and determined the post-vaccination antibody titers. I reported the results to the company and was immediately asked to come to Indianapolis and present the results and to discuss FP in general.

I assumed it would be a small group of perhaps ten people to whom I would present the results. Instead, when I got there, I was informed that they wanted me to present a seminar on FP in general and the results on the efficacy of the vaccine in question before the parent company officials and a larger audience of research and sales staff. The brief discussion about FP in general and the research our lab was doing measuring antibody titers and immunity went well, but then I had to present the research we had conducted on their vaccine. I have this image of the vital slide seared in my memory. The cats with the pre-vaccination titers were all listed as "0," and the post-vaccination titers were also all listed as "0." Just like the unvaccinated controls. You could have heard a pin drop in that auditorium. Here was this kid, still wet behind the ears from a research standpoint, telling this large, well-known pharmaceutical company in essence that the vaccine they were selling all over the country was worthless and did not produce any immunity against FP.

The veterinarian thanked me for the seminar. He knew they had a problem, but the powers that be had to be convinced. The company immediately withdrew the vaccine. We were able to provide them with an isolate of the FP virus that was adapted to cell cultures and provide them with the details of growing the virus in cell cultures. The company proceeded to develop a new vaccine, which was licensed and marketed as an effective vaccine. The lesson I learned from this seminar was that I did not have to tell them the vaccine was worthless. Rather, I could conduct accurate research and let the research results do the talking.

The third seminar provided a valuable lesson on being incredibly careful how you say things during a public seminar, especially when you are representing a prestigious university like Cornell University. This seminar was given during the annual veterinary conference at Cornell. I discussed the information about the transfer of maternal immunity from the queen to her kittens and the efficacy of a couple of new inactivated vaccines that were now marketed. A new, modified live-virus vaccine—the first of its kind—had just been launched, but we had not yet evaluated its efficacy. I thought I had clearly stated that we had not looked at this vaccine, but that there was good reason to believe it would be a good and efficacious vaccine. A couple of weeks after the meeting, I received a call from an official at the company that was marketing this new vaccine. They asked me to come to Lincoln, Nebraska, to meet with key company people, which I did. During the discussion, they told me that after my presentation at Cornell, sales of this new vaccine had plummeted throughout the Northeast. Somehow, those attending the seminar had the impression that I said this new vaccine was not efficacious. One of the company individuals then told me something that I never forgot. He said, "I don't think you realize the power you have in what you say because you are representing Cornell University." Wow! Lesson learned.

Two other special CE programs were interesting because of their audiences and how they received information. The first was the winter meeting of the American Association of Feline Practitioners, or the ski meeting as they referred to it, in the mid-to-late 1970s. It was at the Breckenridge Ski Resort in Breckenridge, Colorado. To meet the tax-deductible requirements of any educational meeting, there must be six hours of meeting each day. So, the CE program was scheduled from 7:00 a.m. until 10:00 a.m., and from 4:00 p.m. until 7:00 p.m. each day, with lots of time for skiing between the meeting sessions. At the starting time of 7:00 a.m., the AAFP members were all there with their notebooks to take notes—in their ski duds! I had leisurely time in the middle of the day to take in the fabulous landscapes and enjoy a casual lunch. I figured I would not see any of the guys or gals after six hours of skiing, but at 4:00 p.m., all the AAFP members were present—in their ski duds, and alert and engaged for the entire meeting. Wow! That was impressive and once more confirmed my assessment that the AAFP members were dedicated to providing the best care possible for their feline patients.

 The second special CE program was for the Northern California Veterinary Golf Association. Being an avid golfer—I did not say good golfer—I jumped at the invitation to give the CE program one year. I can see you laughing already because you know what is coming. This meeting was held at a hotel in Carmel, California, next to the Monterey Peninsula, one of the golf Meccas in the country with courses like Pebble Beach, Poppy Hills, Cypress Point, and Spanish Bay. The schedule of the scientific program was similar to that outlined above for the ski meeting—early morning and late afternoon scientific meetings, with time for golf in the middle of the day. This group of veterinarians were there for one purpose and only one purpose—to play golf. They could care less about anything I had to say about feline infectious diseases. Although we did not play the big-name courses, I had a good time playing golf. I was thankful that I did not have to certify that every person there actively participated in six hours of learning about feline infectious diseases each day.

One major fear that I had in those "traveling" days was that I would somehow forget an engagement or have the wrong time or place. Fortunately, this never happened. However, one error did occur in notifying me completely of the details of a meeting. A major company was introducing a new feline diagnostic test into Europe, and a committee of key individuals was asked to come to Paris and discuss this test and its introduction. There were no seminars or lectures scheduled, but each person was to share his/her thoughts about the topic. The meeting was to be held at a particular hotel, near the Arc de Triomphe, and we were to meet for dinner the night before the committee meeting. I arrived at said hotel only to find that I did not have a room reservation and that no dinner was scheduled that evening for the group. I did find announcements of the meeting there for the following day, so I knew I had the right hotel for the meeting. What to do? I did not have the contact information of the meeting organizer, so I just registered for a room and had a quiet dinner and evening by myself. I arrived at the meeting site the next morning, only to be questioned as to why I did not show up at the correct hotel or for dinner the night before. It seemed everyone but me had stayed at a different hotel from the one where the meeting was held. Somehow, the organizer had failed to tell me, or perhaps I had missed the message. The kicker was that when I did not show at the correct hotel, the organizer called my wife and told her that I was a no show. Ouch! That is a nice way to upset your spouse. Of course, this was before cell phones, email, and text messages. There were also some major problems in how that meeting was run, so this turned out to be a bad experience all around.

Feline Infectious Disease Elective

In the early 1970s, all veterinary students at Cornell had to take the same core curriculum, 8:00 a.m. to 5:00 p.m. five days a week. There were no elective courses; there was not time in the curriculum for electives. Here I was gallivanting all over the country, giving these CE courses to practicing veterinarians on feline infectious diseases, while our own students were not getting the same information. How could this failure be rectified? After various discussions, a one-credit elective course on feline infectious diseases was proposed and approved, to be given one evening a week at 7:00 p.m. It was set up with an S/U grade—students just had to show up at the lectures to receive a "satisfactory" grade, and there were no exams. Perhaps fifteen to twenty students elected for this extra course, and it appeared to be well received. This elective course continued to be given most years, in one form or another, for more than forty years. When I retired, Dr. Steve Barr took over responsibility for the feline elective and invited me to continue giving a few lectures each year. That was how my formal teaching career at Cornell started. Another open door! Do you think the Lord may have been orchestrating this whole thing without my even knowing it?

A few years later, the curriculum was modified slightly to allow time for a few elective courses. The feline infectious disease course was expanded to two credits to cover feline and canine infectious diseases. The faculty from the Baker Institute, world-renowned canine infectious disease experts, gave the lectures covering canine infectious diseases.

Virology and Viral Disease Core Course

The large bacteriology/virology course that had been given to second-year veterinary students for many years was eventually split into two courses. The virology part became a two-credit lecture/lab course. I was asked to assist with the lab portion of the course, which I gladly did. It soon became evident that with the burgeoning information on viral diseases of animals, it would be more appropriate for the students to convert the virology course to a two-credit lecture course and delete the laboratory. After the dust settled, I was designated to teach this virology lecture course, which was titled "Virology and Viral Diseases of Animals." This involved an overview of virology and an overview of the important viral diseases of cattle, horses, swine, sheep, goats, dogs, and cats. So, for the next twenty years, this course was given to all second-year veterinary students until the veterinary curriculum underwent a major change to a case-based curriculum in the mid-1990s.

One of my graduate students, Dr. Jeff Barlough, assisted with this course as time allowed. Jeff was a talented veterinarian and investigator, a bit of a character with a weird sense of humor, and a gifted writer and lecturer. He gave the lecture on rabies one year with a marvelous French accent, completely decked out as Louis Pasteur, the famous nineteenth-century French microbiologist, and developer of the first rabies vaccine. He even enlisted two of the women in the class, completely dressed in mid-1800s French dress, to assist him. It was marvelous, and I am sure the students never forgot that lecture. Jeff also gave a marvelous exam to the students in which he placed the students in an English veterinary practice as James Herriot (*All Creature Great and Small*) and proceeded to take them through the Yorkshire countryside, going from farm to farm and dealing with various viral diseases.

Teaching Slide Preparation

As I was writing this part of the book, I had a discussion with a current graduate student at the Cornell CVM. I was reminiscing about some of the "good old days," and I mentioned Kodachrome slides in relation to teaching. She quizzically looked at me and asked, "What's a Kodachrome?" Wow! I am getting old. This set me thinking and stimulated me to review what was involved in getting a lecture together in the pre-computer, pre-digital imaging, and pre-PowerPoint era. Also, this discussion occurred at the time I was cleaning out my office at the Baker Institute/Feline Health Center. What do I do with the thousands of Kodachrome and other slides? Fortunately, Dr. John Parker, a faculty member at the Baker Institute and an investigator of feline infectious diseases, was happy to take all my old slides that showed clinical disease.

The various methods of illustrating material for an audience in the late 1960s and 1970s were (1) use of a blackboard or chalkboard, (2) use of an overhead projector with a transparency that was projected onto a screen, and (3) use of a projector that would project the slides onto a screen. I never adapted to use the first two efficiently or effectively. Most lecturers were using the projector, with a carousel that would hold sixty slides and a remote-control cord to advance the slides. This is the method that I initially attempted to learn. After each fail that occurred in the middle of a seminar or lecture, such as slides projected upside-down or reversed, you learned how to prevent that in the future. One key was to mark the lower-left corner of slides with a large colored dot, so that when they were inserted into the carousel upside-down, a quick glance at the carousel would show the dots at the top outside edge and confirm all slides were properly inserted into the carousel.

Probably the hardest part of lecturing at the beginning was creating the slides. The colored Kodachrome slides were easy—take color photographs of lesions of animals with a camera, or photograph changes in tissue sections or cell culture with a special camera attached to a microscope. The film was dropped off at a local store to be developed, and the individual pictures were inserted into 2"x2" frames. My early photos were taken with an inexpensive Kodak Instamatic camera.

In the pre-computer, pre-PowerPoint, pre-digitalized days, creating text slides was a real challenge. The text had to be typed on paper and then photographed. A simple photo of the typed text resulted in a black and white slide, which was processed like the Kodachrome slides. Then there were efforts to put color into the slide, such as a blue background slide. There was a lab at Cornell that would create blue slides by a process that I believe was Diazo. Some were good, but I recall some less-than-satisfactory results, like the time a veterinarian came up to me after a presentation and commented something like, "Interesting presentation, but I think you should know, I couldn't read any of your slides." Oops. Fail. Time to make some changes. A classic example of a complication with these slides was slides that looked good in a viewing box in your office yet did not look so good in a large auditorium. This proved another major learning point.

There was also a learning process as to what made a good slide. I recall the American Animal Hospital Association was quite specific in how to create a good slide. One point was that no slide should contain more than twenty-five words. With each seminar or talk, you tried to improve the slides as well as the presentation. It was a continual learning process. You also learned from the slides used by other speakers; when looking at other people's slides, it was easier to categorize the "good" slides and the "duds."

When computers and PowerPoint came into being, it sure was much easier to make quality slides. When everything changed to digital images, I spent a few days at a computer equipped with a slide scanner, turning all my teaching slides into digitalized slides.

The slide carousels used with the slide projectors were rather bulky when traveling. Each hour of talk meant a carousel with fifty to sixty slides. So, a full day or a two-day CE program required a number of these carousels and getting them into a carry-on bag was a challenge. What a change when everything went digital—all the slides could be put on one stick that you put in your pocket!

Curriculum

During the early years of my time on the faculty of the CVM, all students took the same courses and labs. There was no choice or any electives. As the science of veterinary medicine expanded by leaps and bounds, there was great pressure to include all the new information without any additional class time. That meant more material was presented, and more information was jammed into handouts. This took the joy out of learning, and the students became "burnt out." They went into survival mode—*How do I just get through and graduate?*

The curriculum is the responsibility of the faculty, so I served on the curriculum committee for several years. As time went on, several efforts were made to address the problem. Initially, a modest reduction of lecture and lab time was made to free up a little time for electives. This helped, but not enough.

The next major effort was made to reduce the amount of the core curriculum by forty percent. This simply did not fly with the faculty. I was charged to canvas the faculty to get their responses and find out what parts of the material they were presenting could be eliminated. One faculty member, who taught one of the largest courses, responded bluntly, "Nothing! Everything that I present should be known by anyone who calls himself a veterinarian!"

After the personal computer came into common use, there was a strong interest to change the method of learning from memorization of lecture notes to problem-solving using a case-based approach. Members of the curriculum committee visited three medical schools that were using the case-based approach. It was evident the students were enthusiastic and enjoyed the learning process. Could this work at the Cornell CVM? A lot of work and a lot of adamant discussions finally resulted in the faculty approving a complete change of the curriculum. Lectures were greatly reduced, and specific clinical cases were introduced as the teaching tool. Small groups of five students with a facilitator worked through each case and thus learned the important points that each case was meant to teach. Elective courses were greatly increased in number for students to gain more exposure in their areas of interest. More importantly, the students learned where to find the information, and the whole learning process was much more enjoyable.

Cornell was the first veterinary college in the country to move to a case-based curriculum. Individual courses in the core curriculum were eliminated, so my twenty-seven lectures in "Virology and Viral Diseases" became history.

Graduate Students

I was immeasurably blessed to have a great cast of graduate students! Without question, there was an "open door" that brought several of these graduate students to the CFHC, the Department, and my laboratory. These students represented the CFHC (those conducting feline research), the Department of Microbiology and Immunology, and the CVM. Much of the research reputation of the CFHC is due to the outstanding research conducted by this group of scholars as part of their thesis research over twenty-five years. Someone once said that you should surround yourself with outstanding, hard-working people, provide them with the necessary facilities and finances, then get out of their way. All the graduate students were very motivated and developed into excellent research scientists. The graduate students are listed here as a thank you and a tribute to their outstanding work and career accomplishments.

The professional accomplishments of this group of individuals is astonishing! Out of this group, there is now one dean of a school of veterinary medicine, several associate deans of veterinary colleges, one interim vice provost of a large university, and many professors at veterinary and medical colleges. All have distinguished research careers! Several were excellent teachers. One even became an acclaimed sci-fi author of numerous books. To God be the glory, great things this group has done!

The degree(s) listed in bold were obtained while conducting research in our laboratories, with the year the degree was awarded listed in parentheses. The key professional position(s) held after graduate studies is/are listed, but by no means are all the positions listed that these individuals held.

Donald Schlafer: DVM, **MS** (1975), PhD

Thesis Title: *The Reo-like Virus of Neonatal Calf Diarrhea: Fetal and Serologic Studies*

Key Position: Professor of Pathology, CVM, Cornell University, Ithaca, NY

Don conducted his MS thesis research while a full-time DVM student. After receiving his DVM degree, he did a pathology residency at the University of Georgia, then obtained his PhD at the University of Georgia, conducting his thesis research at the Plum Island Animal Disease Laboratory. He became an outstanding faculty member in pathology at the CVM at Cornell.

Jack Carlson: DVM, **PhD** (1975)

Thesis Title: *Pathogenesis of Feline Panleukopenia in Germfree and Conventional (SPF) Cats*

Key Position: Biologic Research, Rhone Merieux Laboratories, Athens, GA

Jack received his DVM degree from Cornell, then continued with his graduate studies. After completing his PhD degree, he held several positions connected with various veterinary colleges and, finally, worked in industry.

Talmage T. Brown, Jr.: DVM, **PhD** (1973)

Thesis Title: *Pathogenic Studies of Bovine Viral Diarrhea Infection in the Bovine Fetus. I. Gross and Histopathological Lesions II. Serologic Studies*

Key Position: Professor of Pathology, College of Veterinary Medicine, North Carolina State University, Raleigh, NC

As a pathologist, Talmage conducted the pathological evaluations of tissues from a study that Dr. Robert Kahrs and I conducted on the effects of bovine virus diarrhea on the developing fetus of cattle.

Yasutaka Hoshino: DVM, **MS** (1979)
Thesis Title: *Feline Infectious Peritonitis Virus. Cell and Organ Culture Studies*
Key Position: Research Scientist, Laboratory of Infectious Diseases NIAID, NIH, Bethesda, MD

Yasutaka, a Japanese veterinarian, arrived in our laboratory just as we were attempting to launch a meaningful research program on feline infectious peritonitis. He developed into an excellent electron microscopist, stayed on for a time after his MS program as a research scientist, and identified several new viruses of the cat and dog. He also identified a coronavirus from bovine winter dysentery samples that was probably the causative virus. However, he left Cornell to accept a position at the National Institutes of Health doing electron microscopy of human viruses, and we were never able to prove this virus as the causative agent.

Bahiru Gametchu: DVM, **MS** (1978), PhD (1980)
Thesis Titles: 1. *Diagnosis of Rinderpest & Studies of its Antigenic Relationship with Peste des Petits Ruminants using Antibody Test*

2. *Comparison of Foot-and-Mouth Disease Virus Vaccines from*

Key Positions:
1. Professor, School of Medicine, University of Wisconsin, Milwaukee, WI — *Suspension and Monolayer Cultures*
2. Scientific Review Officer, Center for Scientific Review, National Institutes of Health, Bethesda, MD

Bahiru came to Cornell and the Plum Island Animal Disease Laboratory from Ethiopia to study a virus that was a scourge of small ruminants in Africa and to obtain an MS degree. His PhD studies were completed while studying foot-and-mouth vaccines. He did his classwork at Cornell but conducted his research at the Plum Island Animal Disease Laboratory.

Richard C. Weiss: VMD, **PhD** (1981)

Thesis Title: *Pathogenesis of Feline Infectious Peritonitis*

Key Position: Professor of Pathology, Dept. Pathobiology, and Director of Scott-Richie Research Center, College of Veterinary Medicine, Auburn University, Auburn, AL

After completing an internship in pathology at the CVM, Rich joined my laboratory for an excellent study on feline infectious peritonitis. He worked out the enhanced disease in cats that carried antibodies against the virus.

Jeffrey E. Barlough: DVM, **PhD** (1984)

Thesis Title: *Experimental Studies with Four Coronaviruses in Cats*

Key Positions: 1. Research Scientist, College of Veterinary Medicine, Univ California, Davis, CA

2. Novelist—acclaimed sci-fi author of the Western Lights book series, Los Angeles, CA

Jeff was an excellent scientist with a keen mind. He was also an excellent and creative teacher. After a few years as a research scientist at Cornell and the Univ. of California-Davis, he turned to his first love, writing science fiction books.

Charles A. (Sandy) Baldwin: DVM, **MS** (1982), **PhD** (1986)

Thesis Titles: 1. *Pathogenesis of Feline Rotavirus Infection*

2. *Vaccines for Feline Infectious Peritonitis*

Key Position: Diagnostic Virologist, Diagnostic Laboratory, College of Veterinary Medicine, University of Georgia, Tifton, GA

After several years in practice, Sandy returned to Cornell where he obtained both MS and PhD degrees. He was employed as a diagnostic virologist at veterinary colleges, first at Oklahoma, then at Georgia.

Cheryl A. Stoddart: **MS** (1983), **PhD** (1989)

Thesis Titles: 1. *Coronavirus and Coronavirus-like Agent in a Barrier-Maintained Feline Breeding Colony*
2. *Role of Virus-Macrophage Interactions in the Pathogenesis of Feline Coronavirus Infection*

Key Position: Professor, Department of Medicine, University of California- San Francisco, CA

Cheryl obtained both MS and PhD degrees studying FIP and feline coronaviruses. She worked out the transmission of the virus from queens to their kittens in a colony chronically infected with the feline coronavirus, then studied the role of macrophages in the pathogenesis of feline coronavirus infections. She went on to hold an important faculty position at the medical school in San Francisco.

Joel D. Baines: VMD, **PhD** (1988)

Thesis Title: *Molecular Studies on Feline Infectious Peritonitis Virus*

Key Positions: 1. Professor, Microbiology & Immunology, and Associate Dean for Research & Graduate Studies, College of Veterinary Medicine,

Cornell University, Ithaca, NY

2. Dean, School of Veterinary Medicine, Louisiana State University, Baton Rouge, LA

Joel obtained his PhD degree conducting molecular studies of the FIP virus. After an excellent post-doctoral stay in Chicago, he returned to the Cornell CVM where he was a distinguished faculty member and associate dean. He then became the Dean of the School of Veterinary Medicine at Louisiana State University.

Margaret C. (Peggy) Barr: DVM, **PhD** (1991)

Thesis Title: *Feline Immunodeficiency Virus Infection in Domestic and Nondomestic Cats*

Key Positions: 1. Research Associate, Dept. Microbiology and Immunology, College of Veterinary Medicine, Cornell University, Ithaca, NY

2. Interim Associate Dean for Academic Affairs, Professor Virology & Immunology, Western University College of Veterinary Medicine, Western University of Health Sciences, Pomona, CA

Peggy obtained her PhD with excellent studies on the feline immunodeficiency virus of domestic and large nondomestic cats. She was the first to identify FIV infection in the Florida Panthers. After a few years as a research associate at Cornell, where she was also an excellent teacher, she moved on to a faculty position and to be Interim Associate Dean at the Western College of Veterinary Medicine.

Christopher Ngichabe: BVS, **MS**, **PhD** (1992)

Thesis Title: *Recombinant Raccoon Poxvirus-Vectored Feline Vaccines*

Key Position: Assistant Director, Biotechnology, Kenya Agricultural Research Institute, Nairobi, Kenya

After obtaining his PhD degree while studying recombinant virus-vectored vaccines, Christopher returned to his native country Kenya where he has held vital roles of research and administration in agriculture.

Christopher Olsen: DVM, **PhD** (1992)

Thesis Title: *Antibody-Dependent Enhancement of FIPV Infection of Primary Feline Macrophages*

Key Positions: 1. Professor of Public Health, School of Veterinary Medicine, University of Wisconsin-Madison, WI

   2. Associate Dean for Academic Affairs, School of Veterinary Medicine, University of

Wisconsin-Madison, WI

3. Interim Vice Provost for Teaching and Learning, University of Wisconsin-Madison, WI

Chris was an outstanding graduate student, conducting vital research on the FIP virus. He then moved on to the School of Veterinary Medicine at the University of Wisconsin where he held key research, faculty, and administrative positions. He was an associate dean, a finalist for the dean position, and interim vice provost for the entire University of Wisconsin.

Liangbaio (George) Hu: BVM, **MS**, **PhD** (1995)

Thesis Title: *Development of Raccoon Poxvirus Vectored Feline Recombinant Vaccines*

Key Positions: 1. Manager, Small Animal Research & Development, Fort Dodge Animal Health, Fort Dodge, IA

2. Research Fellow, Pfizer

George conducted interesting research on poxvirus vectored feline recombinant vaccines for his PhD studies. His career since graduate school has been primarily in industry, conducting research, and administration.

CHAPTER 7

Cornell Feline Health Center (CFHC)

History

A key moment in the history of feline medicine at Cornell University occurred in 1964 when Dr. Charles Rickard isolated the feline leukemia virus (FeLV). In order to study this virus and the diseases it produced, he started the feline leukemia program at the College of Veterinary Medicine (CVM), obtained grants and contracts with the National Cancer Institute, and eventually built the Feline Leukemia Laboratory on Snyder Hill near the Cornell campus.

At the same time in 1964, Dr. James Gillespie moved from the Veterinary Virus Research Institute (now Baker Institute) at Cornell to the Microbiology Department at the CVM and started a program of research on feline infectious diseases. Dr. Gillespie rationalized that if Dr. Rickard was to study and understand FeLV, then we better study and learn about the other viruses of the cat. Several graduate students, including myself, joined Dr. Gillespie's group and studied various viral and other infectious diseases of the cat.

The original concept of the CFHC dates to 1973.

At the time, I served as a non-tenured faculty member of the General Committee of the faculty. Dean George Poppensiek asked our committee to serve as a long-range planning committee to advise him on long-range issues of the CVM, including ways to fund programs at the College. One of the concepts that became evident to me because of many hours discussing the committee's charge was the need to obtain funding to support long-term research on diseases of the cat. Research on many feline issues that needed to be addressed would be difficult to fund through the National Institutes of Health grants or other large scientific grants. If the College were to start a feline program, perhaps similar to the Research Laboratory for Diseases of the Dog that was started by Dr. James Baker at the Veterinary Virus Research Institute, then funding could be obtained from private sources to support the needed research.

I have reflected many times over the years on why this concept arose out of the larger discussions conducted by the committee. The committee had not discussed funding for feline research, and it was not mentioned in the final report to the dean. I now firmly believe the Lord was nudging me to pursue this concept—He was opening a door that did not exist! At the time, I had no intentions or illusions about starting a new program at the College. This was a few months before my dramatic encounter with the Lord, and I did not have a clue at the time what He was preparing me for, nor was I aware of the many doors that He had already opened for me.

Feline medicine in the early 1970s was in its early stages of becoming an important part of veterinary medicine, and a comprehensive feline program did not exist anywhere in the country at the time. The American Association of Feline Practitioners (AAFP) had recently been initiated and was struggling to become a viable entity. *Feline Practice* journal, the only veterinary publication devoted exclusively to providing information on feline practice at the time, had recently been launched. So, the timing seemed appropriate to launch a comprehensive program to improve the health and well-being of cats. But how to structure such a program? Should it be completely separate from the main college and float its own boat as Dr. Baker had done in setting up the Veterinary Virus Research Institute some twenty-three years before? Or should the new facility be integrated within the present structure of the College?

Concept: The Memo

I drafted a memo to Dr. Gillespie on March 9, 1973, entitled "A Dream for the Future," which briefly outlined the concept of a privately funded feline center within the College of Veterinary Medicine. Although I did not realize it at the time, this was four months before my astounding encounter with Jesus Christ, I am now convinced that I had divine help in drafting that memo.

Memorandum for the Record - (A Dream for the Future)

Fred W. Scott, DVM, PhD

March 9, 1973

Subject: Cornell University Center for the Study of Feline Diseases

Perspective: A center for research on diseases of the domestic cat would be established within the New York State Veterinary College at Cornell University. An endowment fund would be established to support research and would be administered by the Director of the Development for Animal Disease Study in cooperation with the University Development Office. An advisory board would be established to recommend to the Director of Development the allocation of funds to the various research projects.

Purposes:

1. To promote research on the diseases of the cat in order to prevent or cure these diseases. It would not include research where the cat is merely an animal model or research animal.

2. To serve as an identifiable unit for purposes of fundraising and promotion of feline research.

The Center: The Center for the Study of Feline Diseases (CSFD) would be multi-disciplinary and would include interested researchers and clinicians throughout the Veterinary College. Laboratories, clinics, offices, and animal facilities in the main college and MRW would be utilized; thus, no new facilities would be needed. The Director of the center would be a researcher actively engaged in research on feline diseases. Other scientists making up the center would be professors, research associates, residents, interns, and graduate students involved in research on feline diseases. They would retain their present department affiliations and responsibilities.

Funds: The financial support for the CSFD would be from endowment funds given to Cornell University for support of feline research. These funds would be administered by the Office of Development for Animal Disease Study at the Veterinary College and the University Development Office. The College Director of Development would solicit endowment funds through alumni, professional journals, cat journals, personal contacts, cat food manufacturers, and pharmaceutical companies. Individual investigators would still apply for federal research grants where possible. The goal for endowment support would be $1,000,000, which, invested with an anticipated 10% return, would provide $100,000 annually to support feline disease research.

The Concept Fine Tuned

Dr. Gillespie agreed with the idea and forwarded the memo to Dean Poppensiek. After input from Dr. Gillespie, Dean Poppensiek, and Dr. James Baker, the concept was tweaked and fine-tuned. Dr. Baker was very helpful in guiding me as to what to do and what not to do with a facility that would be in constant contact with the public and that would be relying heavily on the public for funding. His advice on the name was that it must include the following words: "feline," "Cornell" (for the power that name carries), and "health" (to emphasize the goal of making and keeping cats healthy—"health" was also a better alternative to "diseases," which supplied a negative image to the public). Hence, the final proposed name was "Cornell Feline Health Center." Dr. Baker said that if the new feline program were to be successful, we would have to identify a couple of "angels" to provide significant financial support. Dr. Jean Holzworth became an "angel" to the CFHC, leaving a sizable bequest to the Center.

Also, the Lord was directing this whole process, and He had the keys to open many doors! Praise the Lord!

University Approval

Dean Poppensiek submitted the final proposal to the Cornell Administration, and the university president submitted it to the Executive Committee of the Cornell Board of Trustees for final approval. The concept of a "Center" was not approved—it did not meet Cornell's requirements for a center—but the Board of Trustees approved the creation of the *Cornell Feline Research Laboratory* on February 12, 1974. Dean Poppensiek then instructed me, "It was your idea, now you direct it." That is how I became the "founding director" of the concept of a laboratory (and later a center) to study feline diseases, with no funding, no staff, and no facilities, but with official approval by Cornell. What a privilege and blessing it was to be used by the Lord in the launching of this program and to direct it for the next twenty-three years.

Where to start?

For better or worse, the decision was made to integrate the new program within the existing College rather than develop an entirely new facility off-campus. Since my faculty appointment was in the Department of Microbiology, and since Dr. Gillespie's feline research program was already in that department, the new *Cornell Feline Research Laboratory* was located within the Department of Microbiology. The new Veterinary

Research Tower had just opened, and part of our department was beginning to move into the new building. So, with my graduate students, a technician, and a part-time secretary, we moved into the new building and de facto became the new Cornell Feline Research Laboratory.

With no money for personnel, how could we assemble the expertise needed to conduct a meaningful program in feline medicine? At the time, more than twenty faculty and staff members throughout the College of Veterinary Medicine had an expertise in some aspect of feline medicine—many would be considered some of the leading experts in that area in the whole country. We were not trying to reinvent the wheel, but we had to ask ourselves—*How can we organize this tremendous source of feline expertise right here in the College?* An invitation was extended to each faculty and staff member to become a "participant member" of the new feline program, and most everyone gladly accepted the invitation. This would not be part of their official programs or job descriptions, but merely a goodwill gesture in working together in any way possible for a mutual benefit. The new feline program would attempt to help raise funds to support the individual clinical or research programs.

In 1980, the Cornell administration, convinced that the mission and activities of the feline program were much more than just a "laboratory," approved the name change from *Cornell Feline Research Laboratory* to the original proposed name *Cornell Feline Health Center.*

Dr. John Saidla

In 1988, Dr. John Saidla, a small animal practitioner from Auburn, Alabama, was hired as Extension Veterinarian and Assistant Director of the CFHC. He was instrumental in getting the Annual Feline Symposium for veterinarians up and running and for getting the feline consultation service started. When Dr. Saidla assumed additional duties at the College of Veterinary Medicine in 1991, he resigned from the CFHC. As Director of Continuing Education for the CVM, Dr. Saidla continued to play a major role in keeping the Annual Feline Symposium not only running smoothly but improving the quality of the information presented. As of this writing, the symposium has been held annually for thirty-two years, with veterinarians from all over the country, and even a few from Europe and Asia, attending.

Dr. James Richards

Dr. James R. Richards, Jr., a practicing veterinarian from Cleveland, Ohio, was hired as extension veterinarian and assistant director in 1991. When I retired at the end of 1996, Jim Richards was appointed director, a position he held until his untimely death in April 2007. There is no question in my mind that the Lord played a key role in Dr. Richards becoming a key figure at CFHC. He had a strong faith in the Lord, and his faith shone like a beacon.

In 1995, the CFHC moved its administration headquarters within the College of Veterinary Medicine from the Department of Microbiology to the Diagnostic Laboratory (later to become part of the Department of Population Medicine and Diagnostic Sciences).

Dr. Richards, during his ten years as director, expanded the image of the CFHC greatly. He was a frequent spokesperson advancing the cause of improving the health and welfare of "kitties" everywhere. He often appeared on various local and national television and radio programs, and his recommendations and knowledge of feline medicine appeared in print on many occasions. His easy manner and infectious smile made him a celebrity for cats within the various media. The cat world is a much better place today thanks to the efforts of Dr. Richards.

In April 2007, Jim Richards died because of a motorcycle accident. His untimely death left a giant hole in the Cornell Feline Health Center, the College of Veterinary Medicine, feline medicine and the cat world, and the Christian community.

Interim Director

After the death of Dr. Richards, I came out of retirement to be Acting Director of the CFHC until a new director could be hired. This three-month tour of duty turned into two years. During this time, efforts began to move the Center from the main college to the Baker Institute located on Snyder Hill off-campus. The Director of the Baker Institute also became the Director of the CFHC, and a new Associate Director of the Center was hired to manage the day-to-day operation of the feline program. Becoming part of the Baker Institute was totally consistent with the intent of the late Dr. Baker, who formed the original Veterinary Virus Research Institute to be comprised of a series of species-oriented research programs or centers to study and prevent the infectious diseases of cattle, horses, dogs and cats. The CFHC now has a strong advocate for its mission within the Baker Institute, and the future of the Center is indeed very bright.

What a privilege and blessing it was to be part of the initial concept, founding, and maturation of this feline center, which became a leading organization for conducting research on diseases of the cat and providing information on the health of cats to the veterinary profession and the cat-owning public. It is a journey I could never have envisioned, but the Lord is a master at opening doors, closing doors, and lifting individuals to heights beyond their natural abilities. I was the recipient of the Master's touch throughout. To God be the glory, great things He has done!

CHAPTER 8

Veterinary Associations

American Association of Feline Practitioners (AAFP)

The American Association of Feline Practitioners (AAFP) was founded in 1970 by Dr. Alvin D. Kaplan, a veterinarian from Arlington, Massachusetts. Initially, the AAFP consisted of a small group of veterinarians interested in feline practice and feline medicine. This was a novel idea at the time since there were very few veterinary practices in the United States devoted to feline medicine.

In 1974, Dr. Barbara Stein, owner of the Chicago Cat Clinic, one of the pioneers in feline-only practice, and one of the early AAFP officers, was concerned that the structure of the organization as originally founded was not going to allow it to grow and reach the great potential that she envisioned. She had a detailed reorganization plan, but she wanted some help to present it to the AAFP members for approval. She approached Dr. Bill Hardy, who developed the first diagnostic test for feline leukemia virus, and me, to see if we would help her. I was privileged to serve a very minor part in helping Dr. Stein with this reorganization and later to serve as the third president of the AAFP (1976-1978).

The AAFP has grown over the years from a small number of practitioners to a vital organization of several thousand veterinarians who now make up a key part of veterinary medicine. The original AAFP continuing education programs in feline medicine consisted of perhaps three to four hours tucked into the program of one of the large veterinary meetings. Today, the AAFP holds its own three-to-four day national and international programs, which are very well attended. Dr. Stein's vision has materialized, and she deserves a great deal of credit for the restructuring of the AAFP into what it is today.

The CFHC worked closely with the AAFP over the years. It was a privilege for me to interact with this fine organization and the outstanding veterinarians associated with it.

Dr. Jim Richards, director of the CFHC (1997-2007), was active on the Board of Directors of the AAFP for many years and served as the AAFP president in 2004. He drafted several AAFP Feline Practice Guidelines, and with his excellent communication abilities, he became the voice of the AAFP.

Jim had a major influence on many of the officers and leaders of the AAFP, both before and after his untimely death. You see, Jim was a strong believer in Jesus Christ, and he had the following philosophy: "Preach the Bible—Use words if necessary." The following passage is a part of the comments I was able to share at Jim's memorial service:

> *I would like to unfold a side of Jim that I saw regularly—his faith. You can tell a lot about a person by the verses he underlines or highlights in his Bible. One verse that Jim highlighted in his Bible he kept on his desk at work was Galatians 5:27: "But the fruit of the Spirit is love, joy, peace, patience, kindness, goodness, faithfulness, gentleness, and self-control." Jim attempted to live his life such that the Holy Spirit could shine through him, and these fruits became his personality. Jim would easily and eagerly talk about his faith, but he was never "in your face" about it. He lived his faith.*

I had the difficult task of sharing the news of Jim's untimely death with the leadership of the AAFP. Some officers of the AAFP attended his memorial service, and my comments about Galatians 5:27 and how the fruit of the Spirit shone through Jim's life were picked up and shared freely with all the membership of the AAFP in various tributes to Jim. What followed was an "open door" discussion that several AAFP members initiated with me about Jim's faith. This was a classic example of how the Lord can use an unspeakable tragedy to get the attention of non-believers.

I cannot help but believe that the Lord played a key role behind the scenes in restructuring and developing this fine organization and in orchestrating Jim Richard's enormous and key role in the AAFP. To God be the glory!

American Veterinary Medical Association (AVMA)

The AVMA is the leading advocate of the veterinary profession. There are many committees and councils within the AVMA. The Association holds an annual meeting every July in a different city with a diverse continuing education program for veterinarians in various areas of the profession. I was privileged to serve on the scientific program committee for a few years, helping to develop the program.

There are several councils that address specific areas that affect veterinarians. Members of these councils are elected by the Board of Delegates at the annual meeting. One such council is the Council on Biologic and Therapeutic Agents (COBTA). I was privileged to serve on the COBTA for six years and serve as chairman for two years. It was a great opportunity to work with the inner circle of the AVMA and to get to know the leaders.

In the early days of the AAFP, their annual meeting was held at the annual AVMA meeting. It usually consisted of a half-day CE program. I had the opportunity on several occasions to speak at these early AAFP meetings and sometimes to speak as part of the main AVMA program.

American Animal Hospital Association (AAHA)

The AAHA is the accrediting body for companion animal hospitals in the United States and Canada. It has an annual meeting each April in a different city, and for several years I had the honor of being part of the scientific program at these meetings.

American College of Veterinary Microbiology (ACVM)

The ACVM is the board-certifying body for the field of veterinary microbiology, which includes the areas of virology, bacteriology, immunology, and parasitology. To be board certified, one must pass an examination, and I successfully sat for the exam in 1970. Later, I served on the examination committee for a few years. The ACVM holds its annual meeting in conjunction with the Conference of Research Workers in Animal Diseases (CRWAD) in Chicago each fall.

Conference of Research Workers in Animal Diseases (CRWAD)

CRWAD regularly features cutting-edge research on animal diseases, population health, and translational medicine as one of the oldest and largest international research conferences on these topics. In addition to lectures from world-renowned featured speakers and special sessions on current topics, many presentations are made by scientific experts and scientists-in-training from around the world. This conference is a great opportunity for graduate students, post-doctoral fellows, and senior scientists to share their research with other scientists in their fields. —https://crwad.org/

Christian Veterinary Fellowship (CVF)

The Christian Veterinary Fellowship (CVF) is a wonderful group of Christian veterinarians. At most of the national veterinary meetings, there was usually a gathering of believing veterinarians at a CVF breakfast. As a new believer, I was introduced to this group. What a blessing it was to know that there were many veterinarians across the country that also had a close personal relationship with Jesus Christ.

One of the key persons in the CVF was Dr. George Burch of Indianapolis, Indiana. George worked for a national pharmaceutical company, and his work was to call on veterinary colleges throughout the US. Whenever he was in Ithaca, we would always get together to share a lunch, and sometimes he would join our men's weekly Bible study at our church. He became my mentor and my encourager. I would often get hand-written notes in the mail from him with special prayers and encouragement that he jotted down during his daily time with the Lord.

George was also a public relations expert. He had a small side business evaluating veterinary clinics with regards to appearance, interactions with clients, and employee relationships. He often lectured on this topic at veterinary meetings. One of his key zingers that he always asked during his lectures was: "Is your receptionist a warm fuzzy or a cold prickly?"

George went to be with the Lord many years ago. I look forward with great excitement to see him again one day when it is my time to join him.

A sister organization of the CVF is the Christian Veterinary Missions. Many veterinarians have taken their expertise in animal care to developing countries throughout the world to improve the health and welfare of animals, and thus to improve the lives of people. It always was interesting to hear these veterinarians share their stories and how through their work, they were often able to share the hope that is in Jesus Christ.

In the mid-1970s, we established a CVF chapter at Cornell. It was always a joy to interact with faculty, staff, and students at these monthly meetings at someone's house. These meetings were great opportunities to share a meal, enjoy warm fellowship, and hear how the Lord was working in individual lives.

CHAPTER 9

Honors and Awards

Grace

I have been the recipient of several honors and awards during my lifetime. Without question, at the age of thirty-seven, the greatest was the saving grace given to me by Jesus Christ—mercy and forgiveness of all my sins when I deserved justice.

My other honors and awards I consider recognition of the tremendous role played by Jesus in my work and life. "Let him who boasts boast in the Lord."—1Cor. 1:31; 2Cor. 10:17 *"How could I boast on anything I've ever seen or done. How could I dare to claim as mine the victories God has won."*—William J. Gaither, Mitch Humphries, Gloria Gaither. Just a Sinner, Saved by Grace. Gaither Vocal Band. https://www.youtube.com/watch?v=snjd291QmiE.

Just a Sinner, Saved by Grace

If you could see
What I once was
If you could go with me

Back to where I started from
Then, I know you would see
A miracle of Love that put me
In its sweet embrace
And made me what I am today
Just an old sinner
Saved by grace

How could I boast on anything
I've ever seen or done
How could I dare to claim as mine
The victories God has won
Where would I be
Had God not brought me
Gently to this place
I'm here to say I'm nothing but
A sinner saved by grace

I'm just a sinner
Saved by grace
When I stood condemned to death
He took my place
Now I grow and breathe in freedom
With each breath of life I take
I'm loved and forgiven
Back with the living
I'm just a sinner
Saved by grace

"Championships and trophies are great, but it's what you do with the platform [that matters], because, ultimately, a championship or a trophy doesn't change anyone's life."— Tim Tebow. In the same vein, all the awards and honors I have received are great, but they do not change anyone's life. God is the giver of whatever gifts or talents I may have, and He opened unbelievable doors for me and my family. Therefore, all the recognitions and honors that I have received should go to the Lord, not to me. To God be the glory, great things He has done!

May the Lord grant me the wisdom, ability, and sensitivity to utilize this platform that has been granted me, and this book, to reach out to others—to share what the Lord has done for me, and to gently guide others to a closer walk with Jesus Christ —to change the lives of others for the better.

CHAPTER 10

Childhood and Early Years

I grew up on a small dairy farm in Ashfield, Massachusetts, the youngest of four siblings to Clifton and Mildred Scott. Dad, a gifted baseball pitcher, was a graduate of Massachusetts Agricultural College (now the University of Massachusetts at Amherst), the first in his family to obtain a college degree. Dad was a high school teacher and baseball coach for a few years in the 1920s, but he had a longing to own his own farm. After a few years of teaching and coaching, Dad and Mom were able to purchase a small farm in Apple Valley, Ashfield, Massachusetts, in 1928, one year before the Great Depression began. He had little money but was able to purchase the farm because the seller, Mr. Wing, was an elderly bachelor and had nowhere to live. Mr. Wing gave a substantial reduction in the asking price for the farm if he could continue to live on the farm, and if Dad and Mom would take care of him. With that, they were able to get a mortgage at a local bank for the remainder of the purchase price, and Dad was able to fulfill his dream of owning his own farm. A marvelous open door that the Lord provided!

However, before they were able to get the farm

stocked and running well, the Great Depression hit, and the years that followed were characterized by a struggle to survive and make ends meet. We grew food on the farm, so we had plenty to eat and lots of love, but money was almost nonexistent through the years of the Great Depression and the ensuing World War II. God provided, and I do not remember feeling deprived.

Early Education

I attended Sanderson Academy in Ashfield from first grade through high school, graduating in 1954; the class of 1954 consisted of only seven students. My older three siblings all attended the one-room schoolhouse located near the family farm in Apple Valley, but the new Sanderson Academy (rebuilt after a fire destroyed the original high school's only building) opened two years before I started first grade, so I missed the one-room schoolhouse. There was no kindergarten in those days—just "homeschooling" at my father's side working on the farm.

Probably the most famous graduate of Sanderson was Mary Lyon, the founder of Mount Holyoke College. She was born and raised in the area, attended school there in the early 1800s, then taught at the high school.

Only two boys' sports occurred at Sanderson, basketball, and baseball. I loved playing both sports, and since the school was so small, eighth graders participated in the two high school varsity sports. I was able to play varsity for five years and started for four years in both baseball and basketball.

Church

Growing up, I attended the Congregational Church in Ashfield with my parents, who regularly sang in the small choir. It was always a challenge to complete the Sunday morning chores—milk and feed the cows and clean the barn—in time to make the Sunday service. It seemed equipment chose Sunday mornings to break down.

Students at the local high school had the option, which I took, to attend a Religious Education class at the Congregational Church for an hour each Friday afternoon. I must have heard that you have to have a personal relationship with Jesus in order to be saved and have eternal life, but if I did hear it, it did not register, and I never made a commitment of faith in those early years.

After high school, I drifted away from the church. I was busy with college, sports, marriage and family, and my career. I did not rebel against religion but was just busy and didn't see the need to attend church any longer. I was a classic example of a person who allowed work, sports, studies, and family to take precedence over church.

Early jobs

As I was raised on a small dairy farm, there was always work to be done, seven days a week. Work came naturally to me. I saw my parents and two older brothers, Ed, and Bud, working long hours on the farm. The cows had to be milked and fed twice a day, seven days a week. The barn had to be cleaned, and the hay had to be cut and harvested as the weather allowed. Crops had to be planted, cultivated, and harvested. You just could not put it off until tomorrow. So as soon as I could walk, I followed my dad and older brothers as they did the work. I began helping, or getting in the way, as soon as I could. There were no child work laws on the farm. We cut logs in the winter, and Dad sawed lumber on his old sawmill. In spring, the maple sugar bush had to be set, and the sap gathered and boiled down to maple syrup. Apple trees had to be pruned, sprayed in the summer, and the apples had to be picked in the fall. There was no extra money to pay family members for farm work—it was just assumed that everyone pitched in.

  My first job for which I got paid was nailing apple boxes for the neighboring Townsley and Clark farms during the summer, starting when I was about twelve years old. Each bushel box required twenty-eight nails, and they paid three cents per box. If I worked full speed, I could earn a dollar per hour—big money for a kid. As I got a little older, I worked on the Townsley and Clark farms during summer and school vacations thinning apples, picking apples, or helping with logging by skidding logs with a skid horse.

  After my junior year in high school, I worked for the Town of Ashfield on the road crew. That meant following the grader and picking up rocks as the miles of dirt roads were scraped and leveled. After that was completed, the crew mowed the sides of the eighty-some miles of roads in town—not with a tractor or power mower, but by hand with scythes. I certainly did not see the Lord behind any of these early jobs, but I was thankful for work.

After graduation from high school, I worked on construction during the summers to get money for college tuition at the University of Massachusetts. The first summer, I worked for a contractor who was building an addition to Sanderson Academy, the one-to-twelve-grade school from which I had just graduated. The next two summers, I worked on state road construction jobs, first as a laborer cutting trees and burning brush for the right of way or picking rocks from the gravel as it was spread out for the foundation of the new road. The second summer, I worked as an oiler/truck driver on a Gradall excavator.

As I look back, acquiring the oiler/truck driver job on that Gradall was quite amazing. Did the Lord open a door for me? I had worked on this state road construction job in Cummington, Massachusetts, the year before as a laborer, so when I got out of college that spring, I went back to that same job to see if they were hiring. The company was from eastern Massachusetts, and all the bosses and machine operators made the two-hour drive to the job early Monday morning, then ate breakfast at the only diner in town. So, I figured I could find someone at the diner.

As I walked into the diner, the super that I had worked for the previous year yelled out across the diner, "Hey, Scottie, can you drive a truck?" I said sure, and he replied, "Come with me!" It turned out he had fired the oiler for the Gradall the previous Friday and had not been able to find a replacement over the weekend. So, just like that, I became the oiler and truck driver—another open door. It sure beat picking up rocks all day in the hot sun! That super tried all summer to get me to not go back to college and instead to work toward becoming an equipment operator on construction. He promised me a track to getting my operator's license and tried to tempt me with the lure of all the money I could earn as an operator. Thankfully, I was not persuaded to follow his advice. A few years later, I heard that the company I worked for, with all those "wonderful" future promises, went bankrupt. Another closed door—thank you, Lord.

 Enough money was earned that summer from that oiler position to pay my fall semester tuition at UMass, plus enough to buy a modest diamond ring for Lois. You see, the Gradall is a large gas shovel, or backhoe, mounted on a large truck. My job was to gas up and grease the Gradall and have it ready to go by the starting time each day. Then, for the rest of the day, I was the truck driver, moving the unit slowly along the roadway as the operator graded the sides of the road. The operator would "beep" on a horn when he needed to move forward a few feet, then "beep" again to stop. In between the short moves, there was a lot of time to think as I bounced up and down in the seat while the Gradall did its work. Over the course of the summer, I became convinced that Lois Williams was the person I wanted to spend the rest of my life with and the soulmate with which to share this fabulous but scary journey I was on to become a veterinarian. We had been dating for about four years, but we had known each other since the cradle. Lois and I grew up on neighboring farms in Apple Valley, and we rode the school bus together to Sanderson Academy in Ashfield. We both share the same great-great-grandparents who had owned a neighboring farm in Apple Valley—we are third cousins.

On a Saturday toward the end of summer, this naive twenty-year-old kid set out on a venture into an area he knew nothing about—he went down to Greenfield, the county seat, to look at diamond engagement rings. I found one I liked and that I thought Lois would like. I headed home without buying anything, but partway home, driving up Greenfield Mountain on Route 2, I was convicted that this was the right decision. So, I turned around, went back to the jeweler, and bought the ring. That evening I asked Lois to marry me and gave her the diamond ring. Right after final exams the next spring, at the end of my third year at UMass, Lois Williams and I were married.

We had a three-day honeymoon, then it was back to work for the summer, this time at a large dairy farm in Northfield, Massachusetts, while Lois started her new job in the news office at UMass. This farm lost four hundred cows twenty years before in the devastating spring flood of 1936 when the Connecticut River completely flooded the whole farm and trapped the cows in the barn. A new owner was upgrading the farm and milking herd in order to sell the farm at a profit.

I graduated from UMass with a BS degree in May 1958. Construction and paying farm work were non-existent in the summer of 1958. We moved our small house trailer back to Lois's home farm, just across the brook from my family farm. I helped my brother with haying for a while, but I needed to earn money for tuition for my first year at the Cornell College of Veterinary Medicine. My dad gave me all the logs I could cut on the family farm, and Lois's dad and uncle gave me the logs on a small tract of land next to our family farm across the brook from the Williams farm. I borrowed my brother Bud's chain saw, my dad's crawler tractor, and a neighbor's skid horse Chub—the same horse I had worked with skidding logs in high school. All summer I cut logs, skidded them to a skid pile with the skid horse, and rolled them up ramps onto the log pile by hand using a cant hook or peavey so that they could be loaded onto a log truck. There were no "cherry pickers" to lift the logs onto the pile or from the log pile onto a truck.

It was great fun working with that amazing twenty-five-year-old skid horse. That horse knew more about skidding logs than I will ever know! He taught me a course in horse psychology 101 that summer, which came in handy later as a veterinarian. Here are a few tidbits about Chub.Originally, Chub was owned by my neighbor and second cousin, Preston Townsley. I had worked for Pres as a kid nailing apple boxes and in high school thinning apples and skidding logs. Something had happened sometime in the past between Pres and Chub such that Chub refused to work for Pres. So, Chub was sold to another neighbor, Charlie Nadeau. Charlie quickly established who was boss in this new relationship—I never knew how he did it—and then he just loved on Chub. Chub responded, and from that point on, he would do anything Charlie asked. And similarly, when I worked with Chub, he would do anything I asked—with two exceptions that I will explain later.

First, a little background on skidding logs with Chub. He was a gentle giant who had worked in the woods skidding logs for many years. You first showed Chub the skid pile to which you wanted the logs skidded. After that, he would skid the logs to that skid pile, stop in just the right spot, and take a step back so that the chain could be unhooked from the log. He would do all this without you saying a word to him. You could direct Chub anywhere in the woods without touching his bridle or reins, simply by telling him "gee" (turn right) or "haw" (turn left). He was quick to respond to "whoo" to stop, "go along" or "get up" to start, or "back" to back up. He hated to be led. (Interestingly, in England, the directions for gee and haw are reversed when working with horses.)

Once a log chain was placed on the log and Chub was told to "go along," you just had to step back and watch him do his magic without saying a word to him. If the log caught on a stump, stone, or root, Chub would back up and then pull the log to the side at ninety degrees. If the log still did not come loose, he would reverse himself the other way and try again. Once the log was free from whatever was obstructing it, Chub would continue to the skid pile, stop, back up, and wait for the log to be unhooked.

Charlie Nadeau told me about one time he was skidding logs with Chub on a steep hill in winter with snow on the ground. When Chub started down the hill with the first log, the log started sliding on its own down the hill and hit Chub in the hocks of his rear legs. Chub looked around at the log, sized up the situation, then stepped forward to start the log sliding again. But this time, he stepped aside so the log slid partway by him, and he could stop it with the traces of his harness. He then repeated that process all the way to the bottom of the hill, then proceeded in a normal way to the skid pile. Charlie said they skidded the logs off the entire hill like that, and he just sat on a stump and laughed at the amazing ability of that horse.

One day I had a rather large log lying at the bottom of a slight hill that had to be skidded uphill. I put the chain on the log and told Chub to go along. He leaned forward and tightened the traces, but only gave about twenty percent effort. Again, I told him to go along, and again he repeated his feeble effort. It was obvious Chub had sized up that log and determined that no way was he going to pull that log uphill to the skid pile. So, I unhooked him from the log, went and got the crawler tractor, and skidded the log to the log pile.

Another interesting thing happened one hot summer day when I was in high school working with Chub to skid logs for Preston Townsley. Preston was hauling the logs out of the woods on a sled with his team of horses. Chub had skidded several logs to the skid pile, and I originally thought we had enough logs for Preston's next load, so I casually asked Chub if he wanted to get a drink of water. He made no response to my question. I then decided we needed one more log to make a load, so I tried to get Chub to go back into the woods for another log. He would not budge! I then laughed and said, "Come on, let's get a drink of water." Chub happily trotted down to the stream nearby, got his drink, and then proceeded back up the hill into the woods to get the next log.

At the end of the summer of 1958, I sold the logs to a lumber company and headed out to Cornell University to begin veterinary college. The lumber company delayed picking up the logs for several weeks, and I did not get paid until they were moved. I had to get a special delay until November to pay my college tuition. I do not know why the university granted me that special compensation—perhaps it was just another intervention by the Lord!

While at UMass, I worked part-time jobs during the week feeding and caring for various lab animals—a mouse colony and a small cat breeding colony. At Cornell, after the first semester, I worked part-time during the school year, and full time during the summers at the College. The first job was in the Physiology Department helping with a research project on taste in various animals that was being conducted by one of the faculty.

My second part-time job at the CVM was in the Diagnostic Laboratory, logging in bovine blood samples submitted by veterinarians from throughout New York State for brucellosis testing. The serum was separated and set up for brucellosis testing by a senior technician. New York was in the final stages of eradicating brucellosis from cattle, and at one point there were thirty thousand blood samples stored in the walk-in cooler awaiting testing.

From the beginning of my second year until graduation, I worked for the ambulatory clinic in the drug room. This was part-time during the school year, and full-time during the summer. My job involved preparing and sterilizing fluids used by clinicians during their farm calls. Pharmaceuticals and vaccines were ordered to keep a supply available. Whatever the clinicians needed in supplies and equipment, we tried to provide. Dr. Fox was the veterinarian for the New York State Fair, and my job for him required preparing a truckload of supplies for him to use during the fair to treat the cattle. Working for the ambulatory clinicians was a great experience and helped prepare me for my anticipated career as a large animal veterinarian. The ambulatory clinicians included the following:

Dr. Myron Fincher, department chair, taught large animal medicine each day to the fourth-year class. Dr. Fincher had a few key herds around the state where he would spend a day doing pregnancy checks and any other medical treatments that were needed. I had the privilege of going with him on occasion, and these were great days of being taught by a master. He taught me the skill of doing pregnancy checks on cows.

Dr. Steve Roberts, who taught obstetrics in the third year, was not only a great clinician but also an outstanding polo player who coached the Cornell Polo Club for many years.

Dr. Francis Fox, who taught the third-year large animal medicine course, was a legendary teacher, diagnostician, and clinician. He was also a practical joker, always picking on the students. The students returned the favor in spades, and the pranks between Dr. Fox and the students are legendary. Dr. Fox's advice and counsel was key to several open doors that I experienced in my career. I owe a great deal to Dr. Fox.

Dr. Robert Hillman was an intern who stayed on in the ambulatory clinic as a faculty member throughout his professional career. There usually were two additional interns who covered many of the farm calls, each with a group of students.

CHAPTER 11

Family

The Lord has blessed the Scott family beyond measure! It is with great gratitude and glory to God that an overview of our Scott family is presented here.

Heritage

We have a strong New England heritage starting with the Pilgrim and Puritan immigration to Eastern Massachusetts in 1620-1643 during the Great Migration. Most were strong Christians and left England to escape the religious persecution during the sixteenth and seventeenth centuries. Both Lois and I, along with about thirty-five million others, descend from several Mayflower passengers that landed in Plymouth in 1620, and also from several passengers in the Winthrop fleet that landed in Boston in 1630.

God's providence certainly was evident to our ancestors in early New England. Life was difficult as they forged out a life in the wilderness. Houses were built to protect against the elements, and barns were built to house the livestock. Obtaining food to survive the long winters was a full-time necessity for survival.

God's provisions did not go unnoticed.

There were many positive interactions with the Native Americans, but unfortunately, there were also many that were not positive, especially during the many years of wars in the late 1600s and the early 1700s, when several of our ancestors were killed. One account that boggles my mind and illustrates God's amazing providence affected Benjamin and Martha Wait and their family of Hatfield, Massachusetts. Benjamin and Martha are the eighth great-grandparents of both my wife Lois and I. Their daughters Mary and Sarah both are Lois' seventh great grandmothers, and Sarah is Fred's seventh great-grandmother. The following is extracted from Sylvester Judd, *History of Hadley Massachusetts*. Picton Press, 1993: 177-179.

On September 19, 1677, an Indian raid on the village of Hatfield on the west side of the Connecticut River resulted in several deaths, many burned buildings, including the Wait house and barn, and the capture of 17 captives, including Martha Wait and her 3 daughters, Mary, Martha, and Sarah, ages six, four, and two.

The raiding party, with the captives, traveled up the Connecticut River, raided the village of Deerfield, then proceeded north up the river, traversed west across what is now Vermont to Lake Champlain, then continued north to Canada.

Benjamin Wait and Stephen Jennings, whose wife Hannah and two children were also captives, set out to redeem their wives and children. They obtained a commission from the government of Massachusetts, then set out in late October from Hatfield, traveling through Westfield to Albany. After officials in Albany repeatedly refused to help them, they enlisted the help of a friendly Mohawk Indian. He led them to Lake George, outfitted them with an Indian canoe, then drew a map of how they could travel to Canada. Starting in early December the two men canoed north down Lake George, portaged the two miles to Lake Champlain, and then canoed north down Lake Champlain, battling the ice and wind, finally arriving in Chambly, Canada on January 6, 1678. Further north, at Sorel, where the river from Lake Champlain empties into the St. Lawrence River, and the surrounding area, they found all the Hatfield captives, except for three that had been murdered.

Wait and Jennings went on to Quebec where they negotiated the release of the captives with the French governor, who also granted them a guard of eleven persons to assist in the return to Albany. They left Sorel on May 2, 1678, with all the captives, and arrived in Albany on May 22nd.

Wait sent an amazing letter to Hatfield with the good news of all the survivors, and asked for immediate help of men, horses, and supplies to get them from Albany to Hatfield. They arrived in Hatfield to tremendous joy and thanksgiving and praising the Lord for his providence.

Two daughters were born in Canada to the captives during the winter of 1678. A fourth daughter was born to Benjamin and Martha Wait, who was named Canada, and a daughter was born to Stephen and Hannah Jennings, who was named Captivity.

In the introduction to our family history, I wrote the following about my parents and their New England heritage:

> Clif and Mildred had a great love for each other and a genuine concern for everyone they encountered. Although times were often tough, especially during the Great Depression of the 1930s, they enjoyed life in its basics without frills and with little money. They possessed a strong heritage of their New England pilgrim and Puritan ancestors—hard work, honesty, integrity, love of family, a dedication to help others first, and a strong belief in God. They were truly "salt of the earth." My sister Gladys (Scott) Sellew and I often talked of how God has

blessed our entire family, that "special providence" so often mentioned by our ancestor (our eighth great-grandfather) Gov. William Bradford concerning the blessings God bestowed upon the pilgrims at Plymouth.

The pilgrim fathers had a great impact on all New England and throughout the country. The words of the prophet Isaiah could aptly describe the pilgrims: "They will be called oaks of righteousness, a planting of the Lord for the display of his splendor." [Isaiah 61:3] It is indeed a privilege to know that our ancestors, these oaks of righteousness, were a part of the shaping of this great country, and we, the little acorn descendants of these mighty oaks, give thanks to them.

Generations come, and generations go. Each person is dealt a portion, or a hand to play—some good, some difficult. Each person acquires a certain degree of success and wealth, and then death eventually and inevitably comes to all. Each person leaves a legacy, good or bad, to those who come behind. This legacy may include name and reputation, children and grandchildren, wealth and worldly possessions, and faith and faithfulness. Investment in the lives of others is the only thing that lasts forever."

—Fred W. Scott. *Clifton William Scott and Mildred Evelyn Bradford Scott; Ancestors, Descendants and New England Heritage.* iUniverse, Vol. 1,1-3, 2004.

Spouse

Lois (Williams) Scott and I were married in 1957 and have been married for sixty-three years as of this writing. We grew up on neighboring farms in Apple Valley, Ashfield, Massachusetts, and rode the school bus together. She is the daughter of Harry and Ethel (Dyer) Williams. Yes, I married the farmer's daughter next door, and we share the same great-great-grandparents Edwin and Eliza (Shaw) Williams, who owned a neighboring farm. We both graduated from Sanderson Academy in Ashfield.

Lois is a 1954 graduate of Northampton Commercial College in Northampton, Massachusetts. After graduation, she worked for three years at Massachusetts Mutual Life Insurance Company (MassMutual) in Springfield, Massachusetts. After our marriage, she worked for one year in the News Office at the University of Massachusetts. When our sons arrived, Lois became a full-time mom, plus helped financially with various part-time jobs. She always had a huge heart for the less fortunate. For twenty-five years, each Monday she assisted at Loaves & Fishes in Ithaca, which provides a free meal to more than one hundred needy individuals five days a week.

In 2010, Lois published a book entitled, *If You Want to Soar with Eagles, Don't Hang Out with Turkeys: Gems for Christian Living.* —iUniverse, 2010. The website is: https://www.loisisms-gemsforchristianliving.org/

The back cover of her book reads:

> Lois E. Williams has generated and collected pithy one-liners for the past 50 years, gems that her husband Fred refers to as LOISisms. These one-liners can cut through the froth to the heart of a topic with wisdom, common sense, and often humor. They may give comfort to a hurting person or challenge a teenager as he or she struggles to deal with this world. With these gems, she has guided and instructed three sons and eleven grandchildren and their friends. She is now working on [twenty-three] great-grandchildren. Friends and family have enjoyed and have been challenged by her kitchen bar stool ministry.

Children

Lois and I are blessed with three wonderful sons, Duane, John, and Raymond. All are graduates of Ithaca High School in Ithaca, New York.

Duane was a gymnast in high school and is a graduate of Paul Smiths College with a major in forestry. He owned a landscaping/snow removal business in

Ithaca for more than thirty years, which is now owned and run by his son Caleb. Duane married the farmer's daughter next door, Andrea Crispell, and they have six children and twenty-three grandchildren. Duane and Andrea own Scottland Yard Farm, which includes a variety of animals collected over the years, including a herd of alpacas, horses, sheep, chickens, and peacocks. Many BBQs, weddings, and music festivals, church dinners, and baptisms have occurred at the farm.

John is an eagle scout and played various sports at the club level through school. He is a graduate of Cornell University with a degree in environmental science, and he has an MS degree in wildlife from Penn State University. He is employed as an environmental scientist by an environmental company in Boston, Massachusetts. He is married to Ellen (McCann) Scott, also a graduate of Cornell with a degree in environmental science. She has an MBA degree from Penn State University and is employed by a computer software development company on Cape Cod.

They have three grown children, Zach, Sam, and Kaitlyn.

Raymond played ice hockey all the way through elementary, middle, and high school, and his high school hockey team was New York State champions his senior year. He attended Oswego State for two years and is a graduate of Cornell University with a degree in agricultural economics. He is superintendent of grounds at Tompkins-Cortland Community College, the local community college, and is married to Cheryl (Miller) Scott. They have two children, Cody, and Brian.

Grandchildren

We have eleven grandchildren, six of whom live close by. Two of the three that grew up on Cape Cod now live and work in upstate New York, while the third is a graduate of Ithaca College, and continues there in a doctoral program in physical therapy. One lives in North Carolina, and one in Colorado.

Great-grandchildren

Lois and I have twenty-three great-grandchildren, and twenty of them live within one-half mile of us. We see them often and we must keep the cookie jar filled. Our long, paved driveway is a great playground for the great grands and their friends. We are extremely blessed to have so many of our family close by.

CHAPTER 12

God as Realtor

As I look back over the past sixty years, I am struck with amazement by how the Lord opened doors for my wife Lois and me, providing homes and places for us to live. Although I did not see it at the time (I was not a believer), I now realize He was literally "opening doors" for us.

In May 1957, I was finishing my third year at the University of Massachusetts, and Lois and I were to be married the Sunday after my last exam. I had no money—I mean "zero" money—and Lois had been working for three years in Springfield, Massachusetts, living in a rented room, walking to work, and saving all the money she could. We were looking for a place to rent for one year before graduating and, hopefully, moving on to veterinary college. I talked with a married acquaintance who was about to graduate and asked him if he knew of a place to rent. He said no, but he owned a small, one-bedroom house trailer a few miles from campus that he wanted to sell, and he asked if I would be interested.

Lois and I looked at the trailer, located in a potentially six-unit small trailer park in an isolated, wooded area, in Leverett, Massachusetts. It was an idyllic spot for a couple of farm kids to begin their married life together! The trailer was 8'x28', including the hitch: that is 224 square feet of living space at most, probably more like 192 square feet. It was the only trailer in the "park," and the owner of the park indicated that he was unable to get a permit to complete the park, and we could live there rent-free for one year if I would do some work to maintain the area, including building and heating a small shed over the spring to keep the water pump and water line from freezing. We bought the trailer, Lois paid the $1,700 purchase price in cash, we got married, and we moved into our new, tiny home. Thank you, Lord, for opening the door to our first home.

In early March 1958, I was granted an interview for admission to the College of Veterinary Medicine at Cornell University. It was our first visit to Cornell and Ithaca, and we obviously were complete neophytes to the area. The plan was, if I should be fortunate enough to be accepted, we would move our small house trailer to Ithaca. As we were leaving Cornell after the interview, driving north on what was then Route 13 in Varna and heading back to New England, we were discussing how we could find a place to park the trailer—we knew of no trailer parks in the area. Then it was as if the Lord spoke to me, "Take the next left." So, I told Lois, "Let's take this next road and see if there is a park on it." That turned out to be Forest Home Drive. We passed one small trailer park, which did not look very inviting, and then spotted a couple of trailers in the backyard of a home along Fall Creek. We stopped and inquired of Mrs. Pendleton, the owner of the house and the six-trailer park, if she had a spot for our trailer. We explained that I was applying to the College of Veterinary Medicine, and if accepted, we would move our trailer to Ithaca. She asked how big our trailer was, and she said she had one spot open for a small trailer, and she would hold the spot for us until I found out if I was accepted. A week later, I received my acceptance to the College of Veterinary Medicine starting in September. We notified Mrs. Pendleton that we would move to Ithaca in September and put our trailer in her reserved spot. Wow! Another open door! This location was easy walking distance to the College, so Lois could have the car.

After graduation from UMass in May 1958, we moved our trailer from Leverett to Lois's family farm in Apple Valley, Ashfield, Massachusetts, for the summer. Lois's farm was across the brook from my parents' farm where I grew up.

Our oldest son, Duane, arrived in June. Since there was not enough floor space in the trailer for a regular crib, I built a folding crib so that when it was not in use it could be folded and stored against the wall. That crib served Duane and later his two brothers, John, and Raymond. It is still in our house to this day, sixty years later, serving as necessary for grandkids, great-grandkids, and visitors—the only piece of furniture that has survived our multiple moves and homes.

In September 1958, we hired a house trailer trucker to move our little house trailer to Ithaca. Mrs. Pendleton's small trailer park turned out to be an ideal spot, backed up to Fall Creek.

One year later, in the summer of 1959, Duane had outgrown his crib, and we needed more room. We sold the small 8'x28' trailer and purchased an older, two-bedroom 8'x40' trailer already set up in the Pendleton Park, expecting to live in that trailer for the remaining three years we would be in Ithaca. The Lord had other plans for us—it turned out we would only live in that trailer for one year.

In the late summer of 1960, Dr. Paul Peterson, a staff member in the ambulatory clinic at the College where I worked part-time, approached me to see if I might be interested in a small tenant house that he and his family had been living in on a dairy farm in South Lansing, just north of the College. Paul was moving to Cortland, New York, to become a partner in a veterinary clinic. Cush Murray, the farmer, wanted someone to live in the house who could help with milking chores morning and evening on Sundays when he or one of his two hired men had the day off—yes, they had one day off every three weeks. Also, he wanted a close backup should one of the hired men fail to show up for early morning milking—which often happened the morning after payday for one of the men. These were chores that were natural for this farm boy, who grew up on a dairy farm. We eagerly sold our second trailer and moved into this house where we lived rent-free for two years until I graduated from the College and we moved to Vermont. Another magnificent open door provided by the Lord for a financially challenged young couple struggling to make it through veterinary college!

As far as I can recall, the purchase and sale of the two trailers were essentially a wash, and we paid twenty-five dollars per month for the twenty-four months we had trailers in Pendleton Park on Forest Home Drive. That is a total of six hundred dollars we paid for housing for the first five years we were married when I was a professional student. Talk about the Lord opening doors and providing!

From July 1962 through April 1964, we lived in a large, second-floor apartment in Rutland, Vermont, when I worked at the Rutland Veterinary Clinic. Dr. Don Icken, one of the owners of the clinic, found this apartment for us. After five years of marriage, I was finally gainfully employed with a full-time job.

In April 1964, we moved to Southold, New York, on the eastern tip of the north fork of Long Island. We rented an old ten-room farmhouse on a potato farm. Dr. Jack Hyde, who hired me to work at the Plum Island Animal Disease Laboratory, located this house for us.

Another amazing open door for housing provided by the Lord occurred in August 1965, as we were returning to Cornell where I was about to begin graduate studies at the College of Veterinary Medicine, supported by a National Institutes of Health (NIH) post-doctoral fellowship. In early August, after receiving admission to the graduate school and receiving the NIH

Fellowship, I naively drove to Ithaca to find a house to rent. Lois was ill at the time and did not want to travel, so I was going solo. Much to my chagrin, I found out that rental properties available in Ithaca one month prior to the start of classes were non-existent. I had asked a graduate student that I knew when I was a veterinary student to try to locate a house for rent. The only thing he could find was half a house about fifteen miles from campus. The kicker was that there was only one bathroom for two families. That would not fly.

I had also asked the legendary Dr. Francis Fox, whom I had worked for in the ambulatory clinic as a vet student, to try to locate something for us. He arranged for me to meet a realtor friend. At the designated time, I met the realtor in Dr. Fox's office, and I explained our situation to him—the need for a rental house for Lois and me and our three sons. I had no money to purchase a house, and I was starting a three-to-four-year PhD graduate program. I was informed very explicitly that rental homes, or even apartments, were non-existent in Ithaca and the surrounding area one month before the fall semester. All rentals were finalized at least six months before the fall semester. He did not hold out much hope but said, "Let's go down to the realty office and look through the files."

I vividly recall standing beside him in his office as he went through a large stack of papers listing properties for sale and looking for a possible rental. Suddenly, he exclaimed, "That's it! I completely forgot about this house." It was a vacant, one-story, three-bedroom ranch on Sapsucker Woods Road near the Cornell Ornithology Laboratory. The house had two assumable mortgages, one by a local bank and one by the previous owner. The current owner was in severe financial distress and needed to move the house quickly. It could be purchased with little down payment, just by picking up the two assumable mortgages. We went out and looked at the house—it was a nice, clean house that would more than meet our needs. I called Lois and asked what she thought. We would have to borrow some money to close on the house, but we did not see any other option at that time. We would never qualify for a regular mortgage, but this house had two assumable mortgages! Lois said, "Go for it." I signed a purchase offer, we moved our meager belongings to Ithaca three weeks later, and we closed on the house the next day. The total cost to close on the house, including attorney's fees, closing fees, and down payment, was $1,200. This was our home for nine years.

 Looking back at this amazing event fifty years later, I am still blown away. Only the Lord could have orchestrated this open door! And I was still not a believer, so I just wrote off this event as good luck.

 While living in our home on Sapsucker Woods Road, I finished my graduate studies, accepted an amazing offer of a tenure track faculty position in the Department of Microbiology at the College of Veterinary Medicine at Cornell, came to have a personal relationship with Jesus Christ, and obtained tenure. I will expand elsewhere in this book how the Lord made all these events possible via amazing open doors!

Once we were settled for the long haul in Ithaca after a few years, we began thinking about expanding our house, or moving to another larger house, to provide needed space for our now three growing sons. We discussed with a local builder the option of expanding the house, but this did not seem to be the right option. We had not begun to seriously look at houses or to establish a search through a realtor. However, in the fall of 1974, I began to occasionally glance at real estate ads in the local paper, and over the period of a couple of weeks, one persistent ad for a house in a "park-like setting" intrigued me. I wondered, *if it was in such a great setting, why hadn't it sold?*

Finally, I set up an appointment to take a quick look at the house by myself to see if it was anything that might be of interest to Lois and the family. The day I drove out into the countryside east of Ithaca was a beautiful, sunny October day with magnificent fall foliage colors. The house was set back from the road with a very long driveway and was surrounded by many, many trees—magnificent, tall, Norway spruces reaching into the brilliant blue sky; red pine; scotch pine; and sugar maples in full fall color. It was indeed a beautiful park-like setting with lots of lawns. I met the realtor and began the tour. Despite a detached two-car garage and a wonderful detached 20'x40' concrete block workshop, I quickly found out why the house had not sold. I walked up the outside, exposed concrete steps, entered a small, uninviting sunroom, then stepped into the kitchen. The kitchen was tiny and had old metal cabinets that had been antiqued—Lois and I joked later that the state of the cabinets suggested there had been a calf in the kitchen with scours. The kitchen was dark, and there was only one small window over the sink. I told the realtor that this would never fly—I would not expose Lois to such a kitchen, and I turned around and exited the house.

Halfway back to my car, the thought hit me—*What would happen if we put a new kitchen in the house?* The Lord has an amazing way to give you a message just when you need it! I turned around, re-entered the house, and began to explore it in more detail. In retrospect, I realize the Lord was giving me a "twenty-five-year renovation plan," which unfolded as I toured the house: install a new kitchen with nice wood cabinets and white countertops; remove the wall between the kitchen and the tiny dining room; add new windows throughout the house; remove the "tired" sunroom and add an enlarged, well-lit dining room; remove the concrete steps and replace them with a new entrance; remove the old wood shutters nailed to the inside of the living room walls by the windows; install new carpets and flooring throughout; add new paint everywhere, especially over the pumpkin-orange living room walls; and replace the narrow, dark, winding stairs to the basement with new stairs off the new, split-level entrance. Only the Lord could have put together a vision of how to turn this ramshackle house into a comfortable home. I love to build and remodel, but I am not a genius.

I brought Lois and the boys out to look over this "park" with the house in severe need of a lot of tender, loving care. We had fun fleshing out the "vision." We made a purchase offer, and the owners accepted. We ordered a new kitchen, closed on the house, began the renovations by removing the old kitchen and the wall between the kitchen and the dining room, and moved into our new "under renovation" house in mid-December 1974.

It was fascinating to begin piecing together the history of this "park-like" location. In the middle of the Great Depression, the Civilian Conservation Corps (CCC) obtained about fifteen acres of abandoned farmland and built the Slaterville CCC camp in 1935. The camp housed about 155 young men from 1935 until the outbreak of World War II, when the camp was closed, and the men entered the armed forces to fight the war. The camp had five wooden barrack buildings, a large mess hall, a recreation/library building, and several support buildings. The CCC boys at this camp were primarily involved in the reforestation of farms and woodlands. All the Norway spruce and pine trees on the property were planted by the CCC, and they built the walks and roadways around the property. The marvelous deep well supplied the water for the camp and is still providing water for our house to this day. The men received thirty dollars per month—they could keep five dollars but were required to send twenty-five dollars home to help support their families.

During WWII, the camp was turned into a German Prisoner of War camp with a tall fence around the camp and appropriate guard towers. The POWs worked on area farms under the supervision of guards, especially on the large potato farm a few miles to the east. After the war, the camp was used for at least one summer as a migrant labor camp.

In the late 1940s, the camp was sold at auction, and all buildings were either torn down or moved. The new owner moved the floor of the mess hall to make the floor of his house and used lumber and "trimmings" from the camp buildings to finish off the house and build the detached garage. The property was sold six times—every four years over the next twenty-four years—before we purchased it. One of the owners built the large shop as a commercial metalworking shop.

The Lord in His marvelous wisdom enabled us to obtain this fascinating property and enjoy it for more than forty-five years. To God be the Glory!

In the course of the sixty-three years that Lois and I have been married, we have owned two house trailers (three years), lived in one rent-free farmhouse (two years), lived in two rental houses (three years), and owned two houses, one for nine years and the last for more than forty-five years. The amount of time searching for these seven living abodes was almost nothing. Both house trailers were obtained without a "normal" search, the free farmhouse was "handed" to us, and the two rental houses were lined up by my employers. The two houses we purchased were the only two houses we have ever looked at to purchase! The Lord provides!

The Lord also graciously provided for the timely sale of properties. We sold both house trailers without any time delay or agony over finding a buyer. In a college town, young families are always coming and going. The most amazing sale was that of our Sapsucker Woods house as we transitioned to our CCC home. We were informed that real estate was not moving at all in Ithaca in the fall of 1974 because banks just were not issuing mortgages, or if they were, they were requiring large down payments. We decided not to try selling the house ourselves, and we were prepared for a long "for sale" period. We contacted a realtor friend to sell the house for us and met with him and signed the papers on a Saturday. He posted a "For Sale" sign in front of the house the next day, and the following morning a young couple saw the sign, arranged an inspection that evening, and we had a signed purchase offer two days later. This couple had sold a house six months before, banked the funds received, rented an apartment, and began looking for just the right house. They walked by our house every day going to and from work and decided this was just the house for them. Amazing! The Lord provides!

ADDENDUMS

Sayings to Live By

Your talk talks, and your walk talks, but your walk talks louder than your talk talks. —Mark Trammel Quartet. https://www.youtube.com/watch?v=cNXMoNq7cPE

A Christian's life is a window through which others can see Jesus. —Our Daily Bread (ODB), June 2006

We are the only Bible that some people ever see or read.

Our daily lives are on display for all to see. When our daily walk gives a negative impression to those around us, people are keen to observe the hypocrisy.

Preach the gospel. Use words if necessary.

A life lived for God leaves a lasting legacy. —ODB, October 2004

An attitude of gratitude can make your life a beatitude. —ODB, November 2000

Advice to teenagers: Show me your friends, and I will show you your future.

Give your life to God; He can do more with it than you can! —Dwight L. Moody

If you want to leave footprints in the sands of time, wear work shoes. —ODB, April 2006

Do not expect others to do for you what God had given you the ability to do for yourself.

It is amazing what can be accomplished when you don't care who gets the credit. —ODB, March 2005

If You Want to Soar with Eagles, Don't Hang Out with Turkeys. —Lois E. Scott, iUniverse, 2010

Abbreviations

AAFP	American Association of Feline Practitioners
AAHA	American Animal Hospital Association
ACVM	American College of Veterinary Microbiology
ASAP	as soon as possible
AVMA	American Veterinary Medical

	Association
BGBC (BG)	Bethel Grove Bible Church
CCC	Civilian Conservation Corps
CE	continuing education
CFHC	Cornell Feline Health Center
COBTA	Council on Biologic and Therapeutic Agents
CRFK	Crandell Reese Feline Kidney—a cell culture line
CRWAD	Conference of Research Workers in Animal Diseases
CVF	Christian Veterinary Fellowship
CVM	College of Veterinary Medicine
DOI	duration of immunity
DVM	Doctor of Veterinary Medicine
FCoV	feline coronavirus
FCV	feline calicivirus
FeLV	feline leukemia virus
FHV	feline herpesvirus
FIP	feline infectious peritonitis

FIPV	feline infectious peritonitis virus
FMD	foot-and-mouth disease
FP	feline panleukopenia, or cat distemper
FPV	feline panleukopenia virus, a parvovirus
FVRCP	feline viral rhinotracheitis-calicivirus-panleukopenia, a vaccine
IACUC	Institutional Animal Care and Use Committee
MEV	mink enteritis virus
MLV	modified live virus
MS	Master of Science
NIH	National Institutes of Health
ODB	Our Daily Bread
PhD	Doctor of Philosophy
PIADL	Plum Island Animal Disease Laboratory
ROTC	Reserve Officer Training Corps

UMass	University of Massachusetts
WD	winter dysentery

AFTERWORD

Glory

The purpose of writing this book was to give credit, glory, and thanks to God for what He enabled me to accomplish in life. Hopefully, the tremendous grace and blessings the Lord showered on me and my family is shown through in this book. Undoubtedly, innumerable additional blessings occurred daily that simply slipped under the radar.

To give "credit" and give "thanks" to God have clear meanings and are not hard to understand. But "glory"? What is glory? What is God's glory? What do we mean when we sing, "To God be the glory, great things He has done"? I am afraid I have used this word over the years rather glibly without understanding its depth and power. It sounded good and perhaps exuded a bit of "religiosity" without my realizing it. But it is a powerful word with great meaning.

In the Old Testament, the Hebrew word kavod is usually translated into English to mean glory, respect, honor, and majesty.

As a noun, glory can mean high renown or honor

won by notable achievements; magnificence, or great beauty; an indication of the radiant light drawn around the head of a saint; worship and thanksgiving offered to God.

The meaning of "glory" that I want to express in this book is the "worship and thanksgiving offered to God." If there were any "high renown or honor won by notable achievements" in my career, those should be directed to God for His unmerited favor towards me and the many doors that He opened for me to allow me to accomplish things that never would have been possible by my abilities alone.

The danger is that we might accumulate credit unto ourselves for our victories and success instead of giving credit and glory to Him. —David Jeremiah. Glory Where Glory Is Due. Today's Turning Point. August 11, 2017

On the negative side, many a time when I was on the speaker circuit at veterinary meetings, I was introduced by someone who went completely overboard with accolades and achievements, and in so doing, he/she was "glorifying" me. I found myself feeling uncomfortable in these situations and not knowing how to gracefully handle the situation without embarrassing the individual. Usually, I would just thank him/her for the kind introduction and move on with the program. Sometimes I wanted to respond like the late great gospel singer Bev Shea once responded: "Thanks, but who was that fellow you just introduced? I didn't recognize him."

OPEN DOOR in Heaven

After this, I looked, and there before me was a door standing open in heaven. —Revelation 4:1

I look forward to that magnificent OPEN DOOR in Heaven! What a reunion that will be with all my believing family and friends that have gone on before me! Will you the reader of this book be joining us?

Printed in the USA
CPSIA information can be obtained
at www.ICGtesting.com
CBHW071100030824
12665CB00036B/526